Bahamas

Cavendish
Square
New York

Published in 2020 by Cavendish Square Publishing, LLC
243 5th Avenue, Suite 136, New York, NY 10016

Library of Congress Cataloging-in-Publication Data

Names: Nevins, Debbie, author. | Barlas, Robert, author. | Yong, Jui Lin, author.
Title: Bahamas / Debbie Nevins, Robert Barlas, Jui Lin Yong.
Description: Third edition. | New York : Cavendish Square, [2020] |
Includes bibliographical references and index. | Audience: Grades 6 and up.
Identifiers: LCCN 2018045928 (print) | LCCN 2018046296 (ebook) |
ISBN 9781502647436 (ebook) | ISBN 9781502647429 (library bound)
Subjects: LCSH: Bahamas--Juvenile literature.
Classification: LCC F1651.2 (ebook) | LCC F1651.2 .N48 2020 (print) |
DDC 972.96--dc23
LC record available at https://lccn.loc.gov/2018045928

Writers, Robert Barlas and Yong Jui Lin; Debbie Nevins, third edition
Editorial Director, third edition: David McNamara
Editor, third edition: Debbie Nevins
Art Director, third edition: Alan Sliwinski
Designer, third edition: Jessica Nevins
Production Manager, third edition: Karol Szymczuk
Cover Picture Researcher: Alan Sliwinski
Picture Researcher, third edition: Jessica Nevins

CONTENTS

BAHAMAS TODAY

THE COMMONWEALTH OF THE BAHAMAS IS A COUNTRY MADE up of some 2,700 islands and cays, nearly 2,000 of which are little more than rock formations jutting out of the sea. The nation is spread out over 90,000 square miles (233,100 square kilometers) of the Atlantic Ocean off the southwestern coast of Florida. If all its islands were clumped together, however, the land mass of the Bahamas would fit in the state of Connecticut.

Since attaining independence from the United Kingdom in 1973, the Bahamas has prospered through tourism, international banking, and investment management. Tourism, especially, drives the country's economy. The islands' tropical beauty, warm climate, and fabulous resorts attract thousands of tourists each year, mostly from the United States and Canada.

But the experience of real-life or "true-true" Bahamians can't be found in glossy tourist brochures or online travel sites. The tourist Bahamas and the "real" Bahamas are like two different universes. One is a white-washed, airbrushed fantasy—a paradise of soft sandy shores, turquoise seas, and riches beyond imagining; and the

The items on display at the Pirates of Nassau Museum document the city's history as an eighteenth-century pirate base.

other is the normal, everyday world that lies behind the curtain. Much of this "real" world is beautiful, too. Some of it isn't.

These tropical islands have a fascinating history. Originally home to a peaceful indigenous people, the islands quickly changed after Christopher Columbus and his ships landed here in 1492. The encounter with the Europeans did not go well for the natives. The rapid demise of those island people presaged the fate of aboriginal Americans across two continents in the centuries that followed.

British settlement of the islands began in 1647 with a band of religious pilgrims, and the Bahamas became a colony in 1783. At one time, the islands served as a pirates' hideout. They also provided a new home for British Crown Loyalists—and their slaves—fleeing the American Revolution. They were also an escape destination, ironically, for Africans fleeing slavery in America. In other words, both enslaved people and people escaping slavery settled here. Their descendants remained and made these islands their own.

Today, the Bahamas is bright with colorful birds, exotic flowers, and vividly painted houses; it is rich with sunny Caribbean music, lively dance, and friendly people.

Of course, every country has its problems, even this Caribbean paradise. Some things about the Bahamas are not pretty at all—things like poverty, pollution, corruption, discrimination, and intolerance. These blights are hindrances both to the economy and the society, but they are not nearly as extreme as in some other nations, even in the neighboring Caribbean.

Of particular concern in this nation, however, is the recent influx of Haitian immigrants, many of them undocumented. These desperately poor people are mostly uneducated, unskilled, and don't speak English, the language of the Bahamas. Many Bahamians see the Haitians as a drag on the economy and social services. As often happens in such circumstances, the presence of these unwanted migrants has dredged up powerful feelings of bigotry and hate in some Bahamian citizens.

Church is mightily important to many Bahamians, and the traditional, conservative Christian church leaders exert a strong influence on society and government. Wary of modern values, perhaps, church pressure helped prevent passage of a 2017 referendum that would have ensured constitutional equality for women. And so, gender inequality remains the law in the Bahamas.

The Bahamian government has work to do, to be sure. Prime Minister Hubert Minnis, who took office in 2017, campaigned on themes of transparency, accountability, and tackling corruption. In April 2018, a member of his administration, the minister of education Jeffrey Lloyd, publicly railed against the unaccountability and dishonesty entrenched in the country. "It is absolutely astonishing to me to observe the nature of the slackness and inefficiency in the public sector and throughout Bahamian society," Lloyd said. "It's over; new day, different day. This foolishness that we have permitted in our Bahamian society is finished. You can take that to the bank."

Can the country rise above its problems? The Bahamas is often listed as one of the wealthiest and most successful of the Caribbean nations. Despite racial and ethnic divisions, poverty, and "slackness and inefficiency," it has managed to remain mostly peaceful, moderately productive, and stable. Bahamians have a powerful incentive to keep it that way. With so much riding on the tourism sector, internal strife would keep visitors away—this has certainly happened in other places—and pitch the country into crisis. But then, the Bahamian people seem to genuinely treasure peace and happiness—one could say they bank on it.

The iconic pink buildings of Parliament Square in Nassau are hung with colorful bunting.

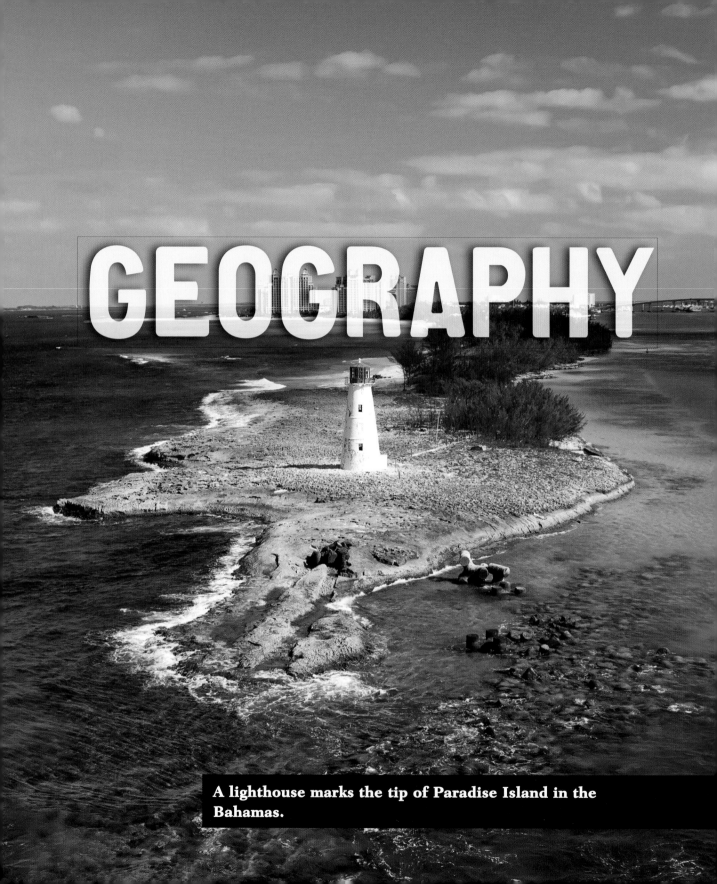

GEOGRAPHY

A lighthouse marks the tip of Paradise Island in the Bahamas.

1

N THE ATLANTIC OCEAN, EAST AND southeast of Florida, a large number of islands barely break the surface of the shallow seas. From the thousands of tiny outcroppings to the larger, inhabited land masses, the isles of this archipelago make up one nation, the Bahamas.

To the south are Cuba, Haiti, and the Dominican Republic, while southeast are the Turks and Caicos Islands. The Tropic of Cancer runs through the middle of the archipelago.

Exactly how many islands there are in the Bahamas depends on whether one counts every cay—a cay is a low bank or reef of coral, rock, or sand—even the ones that are no more than lumps of rock sticking out of the sea. Most references, however, agree that there are about seven hundred significant islands and cays. As for the total number, some sources say there are two thousand, while other estimates are as high as three thousand. Such uncertainty may raise questions as to the total land area of the Bahamas, and indeed, different sources state different numbers. The CIA World Factbook puts the nation's total area at 5,359 square miles (13,880 sq km). Of that, 3,865 square miles (10,010 sq km) are land. The islands range in size from a tiny cay just 1 mile (1.6 kilometers) wide to Andros Island, the largest island in the Bahamas at 2,317 square miles (6,000 sq km). The capital of the Bahamas, Nassau, is on the island of New Providence.

The majority of the Bahamian population lives on fewer than twenty of the major islands. The most populated islands of the Bahamas, in order

The name Bahamas is derived from *baja mar*, Spanish for "shallow sea." The word "cay" is derived from *cairi*, meaning "island," which comes from the Lucayans (loo-Ky-ans), the earliest inhabitants of the Bahamas. They called themselves the *lukku-cairi*, meaning "island people."

of population size, are New Providence, Grand Bahama, Eleuthera (including Harbour Island just offshore), the Abacos, Andros, the Exumas, Long Island, Cat Island, the Biminis, and the Inaguas.

TOPOGRAPHY

The sea around the Bahamas is mostly shallow, although there are deep places such as the Tongue of the Ocean trench between Andros and the Exumas, which is more than 1 mile (1.6 km) deep. The islands are quite low-lying, often no higher than 20 feet (6 meters) and rarely exceeding 151 feet (46 m). The highest point, Mount Alvernia on Cat Island, is only 207 feet (63 m) high.

CLIMATE

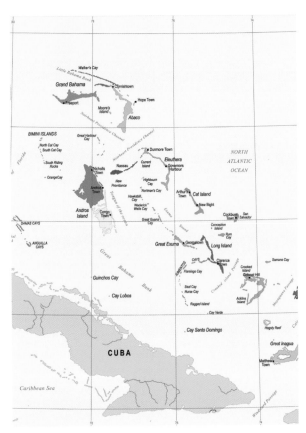

The far-flung islands of the Bahamas span a large part of the North Atlantic Ocean north of Cuba.

The islands of the Bahamas lie in the path of the Gulf Stream, which helps maintain a uniform temperature year-round. A warm ocean current, the Gulf Stream flows northward from the Gulf of Mexico toward Newfoundland. Winter lasts from mid-December to mid-April, with an average temperature of 67 degress Fahrenheit (19.5 degrees Celsius). Temperatures in summer (mid-April to mid-December) rarely exceed 81.5°F (27.5°C), since the trade winds blowing from the ocean keep the islands comparatively cool. There is little variation in the temperatures from north to south.

The average annual rainfall is 52 inches (132 centimeters), and relative humidity is 60—100 percent. The islands usually have only short tropical showers, but for six months, from June to November, Bahamians experience rainier weather; about 80 percent of the annual rainfall is in those months.

The Bahamas is just outside the Caribbean hurricane belt, but that doesn't mean it never gets hit. Among the recent storms that have caused severe damage are Hurricane Joaquin in 2015 and Hurricane Matthew in 2016.

THE BLUE HOLES OF THE BAHAMAS

Though the waters around the Bahamian islands tend to be shallow, there are notable deep spots. Some of these are water-filled sinkholes called blue holes.

The islands sit on top of countless generations of sea fossils and disintegrated coral rising from the seabed. This sedimentary foundation, called oolitic limestone, is a soft rock that is easily eroded by mild acids such as rainwater. Over time, erosion created sinkholes. The water-filled caves are called blue holes because of their color, which is a noticeably different blue from that of the surrounding waters, when seen from above. These cavernous geological features are also found in other places around the world, but the Bahamas is particularly well known for them. Dean's Blue Hole (right), in a bay on Long Island, is the world's second deepest, with an underwater depth of 663 feet (202 m). And in 2002, the Blue Holes National Park was established on Andros Island in the Bahamas.

These subterranean caves may be filled with a combination of freshwater and seawater (seawater easily seeps through the limestone), and some have extensive side passages. Divers have reported a strange orange glow in some of the blue holes of the Bahamas. Scientists have explained that this is caused by the merging of freshwater and seawater. Seawater, being heavier, lies beneath freshwater. Where the two layers merge, a layer called halocline forms. Organic matter sinks through freshwater and settles in the halocline layer, where bacterial action causes it to break down. The halocline layer has a different chemical composition from the other two layers of water; it is more corrosive and typically orange.

Divers enjoy exploring the underwater caves, and scientists do as well. For example, in Grand Bahama, biologist Jill Yager discovered living species of a class of crustacean, Remipedia, believed until then to have become extinct 150 million years ago. On Andros, skeletons and artifacts, including a Lucayan canoe believed to be one thousand years old, were uncovered. (Lucayans were the native people who inhabited the Bahamas at the time of Christopher Columbus's landing.) And in the 1990s, aboriginal human skulls were found in the Stargate Blue Hole on South Andros, during a National Geographic scuba-diving expedition.

With climate change and global warming, hurricanes in the Bahamas are becoming more intense and more frequent.

FLORA

This photo shows a mangrove system in the Bahamas, both above and beneath the water.

The Bahamas contains a significant amount of uncultivated land, due to extensive swamps. Centuries of decay of all kinds of vegetable matter on many of the islands have enriched the soil. As a result, although there is little lush vegetation, some of the islands, such as Andros and the Abacos, have forests of mahogany, ironwood, and pine. Lignum vitae—also called holywood—a hardwood with dark blue flowers, is the national tree. The original forests have been logged extensively to support boatbuilding and construction, as well as to clear land for plantations.

Bahamian plants include palms, ferns, bull vines, and some thirty to forty wild orchid species. Mangrove plants, which can tolerate seawater, grow extensively in the swamps. Among plants introduced in the past century are Australian casuarinas; they were imported to prevent the erosion of sand dunes and are now part of the landscape. Fruit trees such as figs, tamarinds, and plums are also cultivated.

FAUNA

The Bahamas has two indigenous terrestrial mammals: the raccoon and the hutia, a species of guinea pig. Other animals were introduced over the years, and the wild horses, pigs, and donkeys living on some of the islands are descendants of domestic animals brought in by the early settlers. The Bahamian rock iguana, the Cat Island terrapin, the hawksbill turtle, and the green turtle are some of the reptiles and amphibians found in the Bahamas.

THE PARROTS OF THE BAHAMAS

When Christopher Columbus landed in the Bahamas in 1492, he noted in his log, "Flocks of parrots darken the sun." In those days, the Bahama parrot, a subspecies of the Cuban Amazon, was plentiful. The birds lived on seven of the islands, including San Salvador, where Columbus made landfall; but today the population is found only on the Abacos and Great Inagua Islands.

The Bahamas National Trust reports that there are now between three thousand and five thousand Bahama parrots remaining in the Abacos Islands and another eight thousand to thirteen thousand on Inagua. Habitat loss, hunting, and capture for pets have impacted their numbers. Classified as "near threatened," the birds are protected in the Bahamas under the Wild Bird (Protection) Act and it is illegal to harm, capture, or offer these birds for sale. In 1994, the Bahamian government set aside 20,500 acres (8,296 hectares) in south Abaco called the Abaco National Park to help preserve the Abaco parrot population.

New research suggests that the two populations of green-feathered, white-headed, rosy-throated parrots on Abacos and Inagua might be distinct populations. For now, however, the pretty birds are called Bahama parrots, with the ones living on Abacos commonly called Abaco parrots.

In 2017, Hurricane Irma passed over the southern Bahamas, causing great destruction to the island of Great Inagua, which is home to the largest population of Bahama parrots. Parrots are heavily impacted by such storms as the birds feed on the native fruits and vegetation that are destroyed in the high winds. Inagua residents were therefore happy to report that the parrots returned home after the storm.

About 5 percent of the world's coral reefs are found in the Bahamas, enriching the country's variety of marine life. Marine biologists are attracted to the Bahamas because its seawater is especially clear, being devoid of the silt carried to the sea by rivers—and there are no rivers in the Bahamas.

Dolphins swim in the blue waters of the Bahamas.

Capitalizing on this and on the large numbers of dolphins found in the Bahamas and off the coast of Florida, the Wild Dolphin Project was founded by Denise Herzing in 1985 to study the behavior and social interactions of free-ranging Atlantic dolphins.

The Bahamas is a bird-watcher's paradise. The American flamingo, the national bird, is found on all the islands, but Great Inagua has a flamingo rookery (a colony of birds) with more than fifty thousand birds. Also quite common are roseate spoonbills, green parrots, hummingbirds, and herons. The Bahama parrot is a unique bird that nests in limestone cavities at ground level, making it vulnerable to predators such as wildcats that flourish in the Abaco forests. Abaco National Park is a protected nesting area and habitat for this threatened species.

Migratory birds include egrets, wild ducks, and wild geese. The islands are their winter home. Frigate birds, also called man-o'-war birds, frequent the Bahamas—airplane pilots have reported seeing these large seabirds flying as high as 8,005 feet (2,440 m)!

NEW PROVIDENCE

Although it is far from being the biggest island in the Bahamas, New Providence has the largest population because the capital, Nassau, is located here. West of Nassau lies Cable Beach, one of the best-known coastal resorts in the Bahamas. The name commemorates the first telegraph cable, laid in 1892, linking Jupiter, Florida, to the Bahamas. The island has some of the country's major historical sites, but it is mainly the human-made attractions that draw tourists and businesspeople. Nassau International Airport is located in the western half of New Providence.

Just 591 feet (180 m) across a small inlet from the city of Nassau lies the 692-acre (280-hectare) Paradise Island, which originally went by the unromantic name of Hog Island. Paradise Island has been developed into a major resort complex, with many five-star hotels, casinos, and world-class golf courses. About 70 percent of all visitors to the Bahamas land first on either New Providence or Paradise Island.

The Atlantis Paradise Island resort, which opened in 1968, is a huge ocean-themed facility with nearly four thousand guest rooms.

NASSAU

Nassau, in northwestern New Providence, is the governmental, financial, and tourism center of the Bahamas. It has many architecturally interesting buildings, ranging from Victorian homes built by the British administrators of the islands to modern luxury apartments and resorts. It still retains a British flavor. The capital was founded in 1660 and named by its British rulers for King William III of England, one of whose titles was Prince of Nassau.

Among Nassau's numerous historical sites is the eighteenth-century Fort Charlotte, complete with a moat and dungeons. Another fort, Fort Fincastle, was designed to resemble a paddle-wheel steamer. The fort was converted into a lighthouse because of its location on the highest point of the island. Linking this fort to the Princess Margaret Hospital is the Queen's Staircase, a flight of sixty-six steps carved out of calcareous sandstone at the end of the eighteenth century. The Government House, the official residence of the British governor (today a ceremonial post), is an imposing pink-and-white building. The octagonal building that is the Nassau Public Library and Museum was once the city jail, and its small cells are now lined with bookshelves. One of the oldest buildings in the city, the two-story Vendue House, was built in 1769 as a single-story slave market. It now houses the Pompey Museum, a cultural museum named to honor a slave who led several uprisings in the 1830s against his colonial masters on the island of Great Exuma. Also of historical

The Nassau Straw Market features handcrafted items made from palmetto leaves.

significance is the Royal Victoria Gardens, the site of the Royal Victoria Hotel, which had been built in the 1860s in expectation of an influx of American tourists. The American Civil War dashed that hope, but it created another kind of boom for the hotel, attracting Confederate officers, Yankee spies, gunrunners, and reporters. The hotel closed in 1971, and shortly after that it burned down. Its ruins now make a vivid background for landscaped gardens.

The heart of the city is Rawson Square, which lies in the center of Bay Street. Close to the square is one of the largest straw markets in the world, where visitors can see all kinds of items woven from palmetto, a natural fiber obtained from young leafstalks of the cabbage palm tree. Popular palmetto products are baskets, rugs, and mats.

Bay Street, the city's main thoroughfare, contains shops that sell anything from duty-free Swiss watches to voodoo dolls to Chinese silk dresses. Bay Street is also the location of the biggest banks. The capital has become a significant offshore banking center in the Caribbean. Many of the world's major banks have outlets in Nassau that offer a wide variety of banking services to wealthy people drawn by the country's reputation as a tax-free haven.

Behind Bay Street is a wharf complex where cruise liners dock, bringing passengers from all over the world to experience Bahamian hospitality and buy souvenirs in the Bay Street shops. A wide range of boats dock at the piers, from huge container ships to the small mail boats that are lifelines to outlying islands. Visitors can ride on mail boats to the nearby islands, so long as they don't need to stick to a strict schedule (a mail boat's schedule is quite flexible). Horse-drawn carriages known as surreys are a tourist attraction in Nassau. Their drivers—trained tour guides—take visitors around the major attractions of the city.

GRAND BAHAMA

Grand Bahama in the north is the fourth-largest island in the country. The island is about 75 miles (120 km) long and 5 to 17 miles (8 to 27 km) wide. The northern shore is covered with mangrove swamps and wetlands; the southern shore is a long stretch of white beaches.

For many centuries Grand Bahama was visited, but never settled, by colorful characters including Juan Ponce de León in 1513 (looking for the Fountain of Youth) and pirates in the seventeenth and eighteenth centuries. The first settlers came to Grand Bahama around 1841, but another century passed before anyone considered serious development there.

A diver visits with lemon sharks and Caribbean reef sharks on a popular sandbar off the western coast of Grand Bahama Island called Tiger Beach.

West End is officially the capital of Grand Bahama. It is the oldest city and the westernmost settlement on the island. It first achieved notoriety as a rum-running port during Prohibition, the period from 1919 to 1933 during which the sale, manufacture, and transportation of alcohol for consumption was banned in the United States. Grand Bahama Island, being closest to the United States, was a convenient location for the rumrunners, who smuggled alcohol into the United States.

The water surrounding Grand Bahama is incredibly clear, so the island has become a mecca for divers drawn by the fabulous variety of fish and some interesting shipwrecks. Several national parks are located here, including Lucayan National Park, which has a well-charted underwater cave system; Peterson Cay National Park; and the Rand Memorial Nature Center in the heart of Freeport, a bird-watcher's haven with a 1,969-foot (600 m) nature trail through a woods and a pine barrens. The curators lead educational bird-watching and wildflower tours every month.

FREEPORT AND LUCAYA

Freeport, on Grand Bahama Island, is the second major city of the Bahamas, after Nassau. With its twin city, Lucaya, it was created by the rumrunners

The colorful Port Lucaya marketplace attracts shoppers in Freeport.

who made their homes and lucrative businesses there during Prohibition. As late as the 1950s, however, only about four thousand people lived there.

In 1955, Wallace Groves, a Virginian financier with lumber interests on Grand Bahama, was granted 50,000 acres (20,230 ha) of pineyards—tropical coniferous forests—with substantial areas of swamp and scrubland by the Bahamian government with a mandate to economically develop the area. A deepwater port was built to handle the growing lumber trade on the island, and the city of Freeport started to flourish.

Freeport has developed and grown tremendously since the 1950s. Together with Lucaya it has become the second-greatest tourist destination in the country, after Nassau. It offers major hotels, casinos, golf courses, and sport fishing. Freeport is planned on a grid with wide streets and widely separated buildings, giving people the impression that the city is less charming, less "Bahamian" in character.

THE FAMILY ISLANDS

The Bahamas can be divided into three main regions: New Providence Island with the capital, Nassau; Grand Bahama; and the appropriately named Out Islands—all the other islands and cays. The government has renamed them the Family Islands, a name intended to give people a better perception of the islands, one that is inclusive and welcoming.

For centuries Family Islanders led a precarious existence through subsistence farming and fishing, their only link with the outside world the mail boat from Nassau. The Family Islands have their own schools and medical facilities, as well as local government. Many of them are developing their infrastructure to attract some of the lucrative tourist business currently centered on New Providence and Grand Bahama.

The Abacos include Great Abaco, Little Abaco, and offshore cays with a 150-year-old reputation for boatbuilding. The first European settlers of the islands were American colonists fleeing the American Revolution. These original colonists made a modest living by salvaging wrecks, building small wooden boats, and basic farming. In Man-O-War Cay, boats are still handmade. There is an atmosphere of New England in the cays, particularly in New Plymouth and Hope Town, where a style of house called the saltbox is preserved. A saltbox house has just one story in the back and two stories in the front.

Acklins Island, Crooked Island, and Long Cay form an atoll enclosing a lagoon. This was once a favorite hideout of pirates, who ambushed ships passing through the Crooked Island Passage. The islands were settled by American Loyalists in the eighteenth century, but most of them left when their cotton plantations became uneconomical. Since 1999, Acklins and Crooked Island have been separate districts.

The Hermitage on Cat Island looks out to the ocean from the highest hill in the Bahamas.

Andros, the largest island on the Bahamian archipelago, has some of the deepest blue holes. It is the least densely populated of all the major Bahamian islands, with a population of about eight thousand. Except for the northeastern coast, where the bigger towns are located, the island is underdeveloped. The Atlantic Undersea Testing and Evaluation Center, a joint operation of the US Navy and the Bahamian government, is located near Fresh Creek and is one of the world's busiest underwater testing facilities.

Berry Islands is a group of thirty islands and nearly one hundred cays. The islands attract mainly divers and beach lovers. Due to seasonal residents, the Berry Islands can boast of having more resident millionaires per unit area than any other place in the world.

The Biminis consists of two islands: North Bimini is more populated, while South Bimini is the site of an airport. The legendary Fountain of Youth is supposed to be located near the airport.

Cat Island is the only "highland" in the Bahamas, the country's highest point being Mount Alvernia at a mere 207 ft (63 m) tall. That is the site of a small monastery called the Hermitage built by a Jesuit architect, Father Jerome, in the 1940s.

Eleuthera was settled by English pilgrims in the seventeenth century. The main island is a destination for those interested in history and nature.

A small white sand beach evokes paradise on Shroud Cay in the Exuma Island chain.

Natural attractions include the Glass Window Bridge, the Hatchet Bay Caves, and Surfer's Beach in the north, and Ocean Hole and Lighthouse Beach at the south end.

The Exumas are 365 cays stretched over 99 miles (160 km). The main islands are Great Exuma and Little Exuma, and the principal settlement is George Town. Exuma Cays Land and Sea Park is the world's first national park to lie partially submerged.

The Inaguas—two islands, Great Inagua and Little Inagua—have a harsh landscape, a hot climate, and little rainfall, all of which helps their major industry of salt production. Matthew Town, the capital, houses the Morton Salt Company's main facility, producing 1.1 million tons (1 million metric tons) of sea salt a year—the second-largest solar saline operation in North America. Great Inagua is well known for its brilliant pink flamingos, which are protected in a vast reserve, Inagua National Park.

Long Island is aptly named, being 60 miles (97 km) long and only 4 miles (6 km) wide. Long Island is known as the most scenic island in the Bahamas. Cape Santa Maria Beach is listed among the most beautiful beaches in the world, and Dean's Blue Hole is the world's second-deepest blue hole, dropping to a depth of about 659 feet (201 m).

Mayaguana, the easternmost Bahamian island, is secluded. Most tourists who visit do so for the isolation, as well as for reef diving, bonefishing, snorkeling, and duck hunting. The eastern part of the island is popular with advanced off-trail bikers. Ecotourism is also a significant draw.

San Salvador, originally called Guanahani by the Lucayans, was renamed by Christopher Columbus when he landed there in 1492. The island remained off-limits to tourists until the late 1960s because of a secret military tracking station for nuclear missiles. When the US military left the island in the late

BEAUTIFUL BEACHES

The Bahamas has some of the most idyllic beaches in the world. The sand is fine and white and visible beneath shallow, crystal-clear water several yards out to sea. With more than  *2,700 islands and cays, there are countless beaches to choose from. Among the most populated beaches are Old Fort Beach and Cable Beach on New Providence, Cabbage Beach on Paradise Island, Xanadu Beach on Grand Bahama, Tahiti Beach on the Abacos, Pink Sands Beach on Harbour Island, Ten Bay Beach on Eleuthera, and Saddle Cay on the Exumas. They are filled with opportunities for leisure sports and entertainment—water-skiing, windsurfing, snorkeling, and restaurants. About 80 percent of Bahamian beaches are practically deserted, making them ideal for those who enjoy nature untouched by human activity and sounds.*

The Bahamas is also a year-round scuba diver's dream. There are dive sites for those who like exploring wrecks, but the main attraction is the marine life. Most of the islands are ringed with coral reefs—the reef off Andros is the third largest in the world. Dive sites have imaginative names: The Wall, Theo's Wreck, Spit City, Rose Garden, and Ben Blue Hole are some of them.

1960s, it left an infrastructure of well-constructed buildings, an electrical power station, and a paved air strip, which are now used by the Bahamian government. Today, some one thousand people live there.

NATIONAL PARKS

In 1959, to save the country's flamingo population from extinction, the Bahamas National Trust was created by an act of Parliament. As a result, Exuma Cays Land and Sea Park was established—a 176-square-mile (456 sq km) marine reserve for tropical birds and the Bahamian iguana. By the end of the millennium, the trust had created eleven more national parks, covering hundreds of thousands of acres of wetlands and forests, to protect the country's biodiversity and natural resources.

Today, there are twenty-seven parks. As part of its conservation responsibilities, the trust formulates the national strategy for environment and development, makes recommendations for ecotourism, conducts studies of projects such as resort developments that could impact the environment, contributes the environmental component to the national education curriculum, and participates in numerous international conferences.

The national parks run by the trust protect diverse species and at the same time offer eco-related activities such as bird-watching and nature walks. Abaco National Park is a parrot haven, while Black Sound Cay National Reserve is a waterfowl habitat. Conception Island National Park is a sanctuary for migratory birds, a rookery for seabirds, and an egg-laying site for the green turtle. Turtles also visit the Union Creek Reserve on Great Inagua, a 7-square-mile (18 sq km) enclosed tidal creek that is a site for researching giant sea turtles. This reserve is known worldwide as the nesting ground for the largest colony of wild flamingos— about sixty thousand of them.

Plants are important as well. In the middle of Nassau's residential area, the headquarters of the trust is set amid 11 acres (4.5 ha) of botanical gardens

An iguana is happily at home in the sand of Exuma Cays Land and Sea Park.

and two hundred species of palm trees, the largest private collection in the West Indies.

Among the parks, Lucayan National Park in Grand Bahama is special—it has the longest—6 miles (10 km)—charted underwater cave system in the world. Ongoing scientific studies here have contributed to a greater understanding of the chemistry of similar limestone caves. Pelican Cays Land and Sea Park in the Abacos is another site known for undersea caves.

INTERNET LINKS

https://www.bahamas.com/things-do/blue-holes
This travel site provides information and photos of the blue holes of the Bahamas.

https://bnt.bs
The site of the Bahamas National Trust includes an interactive map of the national parks.

https://bnt.bs/birds/bahama-parrot
The Bahamas National Trust site includes a page about the Bahama parrot.

https://www.britannica.com/place/The-Bahamas
The online encyclopedia provides an overview of the Bahamas' land, climate, and plant and animal life.

https://www.myoutislands.com
This travel site offers information on twelve of the islands.

https://www.nationalgeographic.com/magazine/2010/08/bahamas-caves-underwater-blue-holes
National Geographic magazine presents the article "Deep Dark Secrets" about the blue holes of the Bahamas.

HISTORY

This historical photo shows Bay Street in Nassau, the Bahamas, in 1862.

THE BAHAMAS HAVE A RICH AND fascinating history. Little is known about it prior to October 12, 1492, the day Christopher Columbus and his crew landed on one of the islands in the Bahamian archipelago. It was there that he "discovered" what Europeans would come to call the "New World." With that extraordinary event, the history of these islands changed quickly and radically, reflecting the mighty and devastating clash of European and indigenous American cultures—and the subsequent forced migration of enslaved people from Africa to the Americas.

THE LUCAYANS

At least five hundred years before the Europeans arrived in the New World, the Bahamas was inhabited by people called the Lucayans. They were a branch of the Taíno people, who were the indigenous people of the Caribbean islands, and descendants of the Arawak. The Arawak

In 1660, the chief settlement on New Providence was called Charles Town, in honor of King Charles II of England. In 1695, the governor renamed the settlement Nassau, in honor of England's King William III, who was a member of the aristocratic European dynasty the House of Nassau.

2

originally lived in northern South America, throughout the islands of the Caribbean, and as far north as present-day Florida.

The Lucayans had gradually been driven northward by the Carib tribe, a warlike people, whose practice of cannibalism made them very much feared by the peaceable Lucayans. The highly developed Lucayan culture boasted its own language, government, religion, craft traditions, and extensive trade routes. Although the people had weapons, such as bows and poison-tipped arrows, they had not developed armor to protect themselves.

For centuries the Lucayans lived a simple life in villages throughout the Bahamas, subsisting mainly on fish caught with bone fishhooks and growing corn and cassava root for food. They also grew cotton, which they spun and wove into hammocks. These attracted the attention of the first Europeans to visit the Bahamas, as hammocks provided a comfortable alternative to the hard decks of their ships.

The Lucayans traveled in big canoes carved out of mahogany logs. In 1996, boat captain Bob Gascoine was working in a mangrove swamp at North Creek on Grand Turk Island. Suddenly, the propeller of his boat struck a submerged object. Curious, he investigated the sound and found he had run over what looked like an odd reddish stick poking out of the mud. An amateur archaeologist, Gascoine recognized that this was not a stick but a Lucayan canoe paddle. He notified museum officials, and the paddle was removed to a protected environment. It has been dated to between 995 and 1235 CE, and is now displayed at the Turks & Caicos National Museum. The only other Lucayan paddle ever found, in 1912, is now housed at the Smithsonian in Washington, DC.

CHRISTOPHER COLUMBUS

On October 12, 1492, the explorer Christopher Columbus stepped ashore on a little island that the Lucayans called *Guana-hani*. He immediately renamed it San Salvador and claimed it for Spain. The Lucayans welcomed Columbus and his men, in whom they saw no threat. In fact, initially there was no threat, because the coral islands had no economic value to the Europeans. Columbus was looking for gold and a passage to China.

After some time on the islands, which he later described as being among the most beautiful he had ever seen, Columbus sailed south toward Cuba and then southeast to Hispaniola (the island that is now home to Haiti and Dominican Republic). At the time of Columbus's arrival in 1492, there were five Taíno kingdoms and territories on Hispaniola.

This illustration from 1890 is an idealized portrayal of Christopher Columbus claiming the island of San Salvador for Spain.

Unfortunately for the indigenous island people, Columbus's expedition discovered gold on Hispaniola. Before the gold was exhausted, however, the Taíno natives died from overwork at the hands of the Spanish or of foreign diseases against which they had little immunity. Remembering the Lucayans, the Spanish sent an expedition to San Salvador to round them up and bring them to Hispaniola. About twenty thousand Lucayans were killed for resisting or subdued and shipped to Hispaniola to work. Approximately twenty-five years after Columbus discovered San Salvador, the Lucayan society in the Bahamas no longer existed.

SLEEPING ISLANDS

After Columbus's visit, the Bahamian islands came under the nominal control of Spain, an arrangement formalized under the Treaty of Tordesillas between Spain and Portugal in 1494. The Treaty of Tordesillas divided the "newly discovered" lands outside Europe between the two countries along a meridian about halfway between the Cape Verde Islands (already Portuguese), off the west coast of Africa, and the islands "discovered" by Columbus on his first voyage. These islands were named in the treaty as Cipangu and Antilia (Cuba and Hispaniola) and claimed by Spain. The lands to the east would belong to Portugal and the lands to the west to Spain.

For more than a century, however, the Bahamian islands were seldom visited, much less settled. From time to time, explorers would wander into the shallow seas, then move on. One such visitor was Juan Ponce de León, a

Spanish conqueror looking for the fabled Fountain of Youth. Other Europeans passed through, including the Dutch and the French. British explorers such as John Cabot and John Hawkins also visited the Bahamas during the 1500s, but they too did not stay. All these explorers were very likely discouraged by the treacherous reefs surrounding many of the islands.

It was not until 1629 that anyone thought seriously about settling the Bahamas. In that year, ignoring the Spanish claim, King Charles I of England granted to his attorney general, Sir Robert Heath, the right to establish settlements in territories in America including "Bahama" and all the islands lying south or near the continent. This right was never exercised; the islands were too far away, and besides, Charles I had major problems in England, which ended with his execution in 1649. (Robert Heath fled to France.)

Meanwhile, conflict between the Puritans and the Anglican Church in England caused the Puritans to leave for North America and other territories, among them the Bermuda islands, which England had colonized in 1612.

THE ELEUTHERAN ADVENTURERS

Old World religious influence soon reached the New World, and in the Bermudas some oppressed Puritans decided it was time to move on. In 1647, William Sayle formed the Company of Eleutheran Adventurers, whose goal was to look for an island where they would be free to establish plantations and worship as they wished. In the summer of 1648, Sayle and seventy other Puritans arrived at what is now Governor's Harbour on the island of Cigatoo, now known as Eleuthera, and became the first group of Europeans to take up residence in the Bahamas.

The newcomers had a rocky start. Even before they arrived, one of their two ships was wrecked. They sent the other ship out for provisions. To survive in the long term, however, they needed more than provisions. Rich soil was necessary for farming, but the island's coralline base was covered by only a thin layer of poor soil. Consequently, many of their farming projects failed. For a few years, Sayle traveled in search of funds. Fellow Puritans who had settled in the new colony of Massachusetts on the American mainland collected funds in exchange for amber and timber. The Eleutheran Adventurers also survived by scavenging from the numerous vessels wrecked on the coral reefs surrounding the island. Despite their efforts, the settlement could not survive. About ten years after they first landed, most of the Eleutheran Adventurers had returned to Bermuda, among them William Sayle.

Meanwhile, another group of Bermudans arrived on New Providence, west of Eleuthera, in 1656. The soil there was a little better. Quite independent of this, Sayle had also been interested in New Providence, having sheltered there during one of his northward journeys. In 1663, when he was appointed governor of South Carolina, he took every opportunity to speak glowingly to the British about the Bahamas. As a result, in 1670 the Duke of Albemarle and five other Englishmen were granted proprietorship of the islands by King Charles II. They appointed a governor in 1671, then left the islands to their fate, contributing nothing to development beyond a succession of governors who were lazy and corrupt.

The year 1671 was also the first time a census was ever taken in the Bahamas. There were 1,097 residents, 443 of whom were originally slaves brought in from Africa to work on the British cotton, tobacco, sugarcane, and sisal plantations.

The neglect of the British proprietors left the islands open to attack by pirates. Given little protection, many of the settlers fled, leaving the Bahamian islands wide open once again to anyone who wanted to live there. Many pirates actually settled on the islands.

PIRACY

The protected bays throughout the Bahamian islands were ideal places to conceal pirate ships and intercept passing vessels. The British governors who were supposed to be enforcing the law were often in league with the pirates, including such notorious characters as Edward Thatch (Blackbeard), Mary Read, and Anne Bonny. There was no significant change for the next thirty years. If anything, the situation worsened, as Nassau was attacked a few times by the Spanish in retaliation for the loss of ships to pirates.

WOODES ROGERS AND THE PIRATES

Woodes Rogers *(ca.1679–1732), an English sea captain, became a pirate buster when he assumed command of an expedition sponsored by merchants of Bristol, England, to eliminate piracy and make the shipping routes safe for their trading vessels. In 1709, his ship rescued a man called Alexander Selkirk from the Pacific island on which he had been marooned for four years; this adventure inspired Daniel Defoe to write the classic story* Robinson Crusoe.

Captain Woodes Rogers and his men steal jewels from women in the neighborhood of Guiaquil.

In 1718, the king of England appointed Rogers governor of the Bahamas with a specific command: to rid the islands of nearly two thousand pirates who lived there. Rogers succeeded in this difficult task. In 1729, he called the first meeting of the House of Assembly, which passed twelve Acts of Parliament designed to bring law and order to the islands of the Bahamas. By the time he died in the Bahamas in 1732, the days of pirate control of the islands were over.

Rogers himself had been a privateer, so he knew what—and who—he was dealing with. There wasn't much difference between privateers and pirates, except that the first were seamen on privately owned ships who were commissioned by governments to attack—and steal from—enemy shipping vessels, especially during wartime. In other words, they were legalized pirates. Typically they would turn the loot over to their sponsors, keeping a cut for themselves, of course.

Pirates, on the other hand, were—and still are—people who (illegally) attack and rob ships at sea.

Edward Thatch *(or Teach, ca.1680–1718), infamously known as the fearsome pirate Blackbeard, began his seafaring career as a privateer but went rogue. Blackbeard and his crew terrorized the Caribbean and southern US Atlantic coastal waters during the "Golden Age of Piracy" in the early eighteenth century. His ship, the* Queen Anne's Revenge, *was itself a stolen vessel. Originally an Englishman, Thatch lived in the Bahamas, where he took cover in Nassau along with many other scoundrels.*

Thatch was a deliberately scary-looking character with a fierce reputation for fighting, but his buccaneer career was short-lived. He was killed in a sea battle off Ocracoke Island, part of North Carolina's Outer Banks region, by Lieutenant Robert Maynard of Virginia. In victory, Maynard hung Thatch's severed head from his ship's bowsprit.

Over the years, Blackbeard has grown more famous than he was in life, and he is usually portrayed as a monster. But in fact there is no evidence of him actually killing anyone during his pirating days. In 1996, the sunken remains of Queen Anne's Revenge were discovered on the seabed near Beaufort Inlet, North Carolina. The site has been added to the US National Register of Historic Places.

Anne Bonny (ca.1698–ca.1782) was born in County Cork, Ireland. She came to North America when her father, a lawyer, moved his family to the Carolinas to start a plantation. At a quite young age she married a sailor, James Bonny, who took her to the Bahamas where he worked for Governor Woodes Rogers in the fight against piracy.

Anne fell in love with one of the enemy, the pirate John Rackham, who went by the name Calico Jack. Late one night Calico Jack and Anne Bonny stole a ship moored in the Nassau harbor and sailed away to begin a life of piracy together. She dressed like a man, became an expert with the pistol and the cutlass, and came to be considered as dangerous as any male pirate.

In 1720, Calico Jack's ship, the Revenge, was attacked by a British vessel, and all its crew, including Anne Bonny and fellow pirate Mary Read, were captured. Bonny and Read were sentenced to death, but both confessed to their gender and were spared an immediate hanging due to the fact that they were pregnant. Mary Read died in jail, but Anne Bonny, after several postponements of her execution, simply disappeared. What happened to her remains unknown, but most historians think her father managed to arrange her escape and that she returned to the Carolinas to live out her life under an assumed name.

A CROWN COLONY

The settlers from Britain made a case for Crown control, and they succeeded in 1717 when the proprietors surrendered their rights to King George I of Britain. In 1718, Captain Woodes Rogers was appointed the first royal governor of the Bahamas.

By this time more than one thousand pirates were living on New Providence alone. Rogers began the long and difficult task of getting rid of them. His method was ingenious: he pardoned some of them to get their cooperation so that he could capture others. Some pirates were sent to England for trial, and some were executed in the Bahamas, but by 1732, when Rogers died in Nassau, the situation was finally under control, and the settlers could begin to live and work without the constant fear of attack from either the Spanish or the pirates. In 1741 there were more than two thousand settlers in the Bahamas.

Rogers also ordered strong forts to be built to repel attacks from ships. He used these effectively against the Spanish in 1720. In 1729, Rogers organized an assembly of representatives to govern the islands. Thus began more orderly government and the beginning of commerce.

THE LOYALISTS ARRIVE

The American Revolution brought significant changes to the peaceful Bahamian islands. When the war ended with the British defeat, many of the settlers in the former British colonies of North America immigrated to neighboring areas still controlled by the British. They were known as Loyalists because they had supported the English king. After Canada, the Bahamas was the most popular destination because of its warm climate and its proximity to the United States. As a result, the population of the islands tripled during the 1780s with the arrival of more than eight thousand Loyalists and their slaves.

The Loyalist settlers were mostly farming people from the southern United States. With their arrival, new cotton plantations began to spring up in the Bahamas, worked by the slaves they brought with them.

SLAVERY

By far, most of today's Bahamian citizens are descended from enslaved African people. The first such people were brought to the Bahamas with the Eleutheran Adventurers in the 1640s. Later, in the 1780s, many more Africans were brought to the islands by the American Loyalists fleeing the United States after the War of Independence.

Slaves work on a Bahamian sugar plantation in this nineteenth-century illustration.

Throughout the Caribbean islands, stolen African people were forced to work in brutal heat on plantations. By the start of the 1800s, the slave population in the Bahamas had increased to more than twelve thousand people, with black people now making up the majority of Bahamian residents—the ratio of blacks to whites being about two to one.

The British abolished the slave trade in 1807, and existing slaves were emancipated throughout the colonies in 1834—thirty-one years before slavery would be banned in the United States. With its close proximity to the Southern coastal states, the Bahamas served as a destination for escaped American slaves. In 1823, some 300 African and Seminole slaves escaped in a mass flight from Florida, aided by Bahamians in twenty-seven sloops and additional canoes. And in 1841, 135 enslaved Africans found freedom in the Bahamas after staging a rebellion aboard the Creole, a ship transporting enslaved people from Richmond, Virginia, to the slave markets in New Orleans. It has been called the most successful slave revolt in US history.

After slavery was abolished in the islands, life for the freed Africans wasn't easy. Many tried to subsist by farming small plots of land. Others became indentured servants to wealthier landowners. Africans, along with Native American and mixed-race people from Haiti and other parts of the Caribbean, continued to migrate to the Bahamas.

However, the plantations did not prosper, mainly due to the chenille bug and soil exhaustion.

Many settlers eventually emigrated, some to resettle on more fertile British Caribbean islands such as Barbados, others to return to the United States. Those who stayed eventually did quite well for themselves by branching into other occupations, including fishery and boatbuilding. Remnants of Loyalist communities are still found on the islands, their homes in the architectural styles they brought with them. Several Bahamian family names can be traced to the Loyalist settlers. In the Exumas, for example, many residents are called Rolle after their enslaved ancestors who adopted the name of their master, Denys Rolle.

BLOCKADE RUNNING

For most of the nineteenth century, the Bahamian islands were tranquil, although not very prosperous owing to few trading prospects. Most families lived on subsistence farming. The outbreak of the American Civil War in 1861 brought a new opportunity—blockade running, which became a very profitable business.

Early in the Civil War, President Abraham Lincoln imposed a blockade on the American South to starve it into submission. The Bahamians supplied the Southern states with the manufactured goods they needed but could no longer obtain through the Northern ports of the United States. At the same time, Bahamians marketed the cotton exports of these states in Nassau. Many Bahamians had special fast ships built to make their fortunes evading the gunships of the Yankee army enforcing the blockade. The Royal Victoria Hotel, which had just been built to house an expected influx of American tourists to Nassau, instead became a center for the blockade runners and quickly earned a reputation as the place to party every night.

The excitement and prosperity of the Civil War years ended with the surrender of the Confederacy in 1865, and the Bahamas returned to its peaceful existence. New opportunities emerged only to fail. For example, conch (KONK) shells became a good trade item for a while until the fashion for them died. The trade in sea sponges prospered until they were all killed by a fungus. In addition, the invention of synthetic substitutes sharply reduced demand for natural sponges. Pineapple-canning factories, which had been established in the Bahamas with high expectations, began to fail after the American government put a punitive import tax on pineapples entering the United States. The citrus fruit crops met the same fate.

This 1864 print from the *Illustrated London News* shows workers in Nassau unloading cotton from blockade runners during the American Civil War.

World War I (1914—1918) further damaged the economy of the islands, which was still strongly linked to Britain's economy. The Bahamas had little real contact with the war, but the people proved themselves to be British patriots by contributing lives and funds to the war effort.

PROHIBITION BOOM

As Florida began to develop, many Bahamians left to settle there, with mixed results for the Bahamas. On the positive side, new communication links were established with the booming city of Miami—first a regular steamship service, then a telegraph connection, and after 1931, radio links. One negative result was the depletion of the population in the Bahamas.

Salvation, in a sense, came in 1919 with the advent of Prohibition, a period when alcohol was banned in the United States. For the next fourteen years, the Bahamas supplied illegal alcohol to speakeasies (places selling drinks illegally) all over the United States. The good old days of blockade running began again, and many Bahamians made fortunes operating small, fast boats that outran the US Coast Guard and delivered whisky, gin, rum, and beer to the many inlets dotting the eastern Florida coast. When Prohibition ended in 1933, the Bahamas succumbed to the Great Depression—a ten-year worldwide economic crisis that had begun in 1929.

A TAX REFUGE

One of the world's wealthiest men came to the rescue. In 1934, Sir Harry Oakes, an American-born British baronet and Canadian gold mine owner, moved to the Bahamas. He found it a good place to live, both for its climate and for its hands-off attitude toward the taxes he should have been paying on his fortune. He told his friends about this attractive tax haven, and the Bahamas began to gain popularity among the wealthy for permanent residence. Among those who could not afford to live there, it became known as a beautiful place to visit.

The appointment of the Duke of Windsor as the governor of the Bahamas in 1940 added to the attraction of the Bahamas during World War II, for the duke was a popular man. He was the former king of England, Edward VIII, who had abdicated the throne in 1936 to marry an American divorcée. He instituted economic reforms and was instrumental in the building of an

The Duke of Windsor, as the governor of the Bahamas, visits with farm laborers during World War II.

air base on New Providence to train pilots during the war. The Bahamas also became important as a strategic base for antisubmarine warfare against the Germans. Two airports built during the war to support the Allied forces based there later provided the infrastructure for the postwar tourism boom.

After the war ended, the Bahamians took advantage of the facilities left behind by the British to develop the tourist industry. This was timely, for by then the attitude of the middle classes to leisure had changed, and more people who were not rich were traveling for pleasure. Then, in the early 1960s, after Cuba became a communist nation and the United States imposed an embargo on that country, tourists looking for a new destination discovered the perfect alternative in the Bahamas.

INDEPENDENCE

The Bahamians had been in control of their internal government since Woodes Rogers established an assembly of representatives in 1729, but sovereignty was still held by the British Crown. This meant that the Bahamas

Though it occurred in 1943, the murder of Sir Harry Oakes was so shocking it was quickly dubbed the "crime of the century." In the Bahamas, certainly, it may well have been— and it remains unsolved to this day.

Oakes was the colony's wealthiest, most powerful, high-profile resident; he owned about one third of New Providence Island. Born in Maine, he'd made his fortune in Canadian gold mines and was awarded the British aristocratic title of baronet in recognition of his charitable donations. He played a major role in developing the sleepy backwater Bahamas into a destination location.

On the night of July 7, Oakes was found gruesomely murdered in his bedroom at Westbourne, the mansion on his huge Bahamian estate. At the time, his wife and children were in Maine, and a tropical storm was raging across the Caribbean. The crime was especially gristly and the murder scene was full of evidence, but the detectives did little to investigate. The governor of the Bahamas, the Duke of Windsor, appeared reluctant to pursue the case.

Although there were plenty of possible suspects—Oakes had many enemies—the murder was quickly pinned on Oakes's son-in-law, Count Alfred de Marigny. A court case ensued, and de Marigny was acquitted after it was revealed that evidence had been planted by the police and the defendant was being framed. No other suspect was ever brought in, as the governor ordered the investigation stopped.

All these years later, the murder remains unsolved, though plenty of juicy whodunnit theories have been posited in books and movies. Sir Harry Oakes, once the Bahamas' greatest citizen, remains its greatest mystery.

FATHER OF THE NATION

Sir Lynden Pindling (1930–2000), the "father of independence," served as the first black premier of the Bahamas from 1967 to 1969, ending the tradition of white minority rule that had been in place for centuries. He helped lead his country to independence and went on to become the nation's prime minister from 1969 to 1992, as well as the leader of the Progressive Liberal Party (PLP).

Despite his early political devotion to fighting gambling, corruption, and organized crime, Pindling eventually faced serious allegations of corruption, including dealings with US mob leaders involved with the casino industry. In 1983, an American investigative report claimed Pindling was deeply implicated in allowing the notorious Medellin Cartel access to Bahamian ports as safe passage points for US-bound cocaine and marijuana from South America. The prime minister was accused of accepting millions of dollars in bribes, far in excess of his salary. Although subsequent investigations found evidence of widespread corruption among Bahamian government officials and police, Pindling himself was cleared, though the source of his wealth was never explained.

The prime minister maintained high popularity, particularly among older Bahamians, and continues to be revered as the "father of the nation." In 2006, the Nassau International Airport was renamed in his honor, as the Lynden Pindling International Airport. His image is also depicted on the Bahamian one-dollar note.

In 2014, his widow, Marguerite Pindling was named governor-general of the Commonwealth of the Bahamas.

was a colony of the British Empire, but its own politicians were able to make most decisions with regards to the running of the Bahamas without reference to the British Crown. In 1963, during a conference in London, it was agreed that the Bahamas should be given self-government. The process began with a new constitution in 1964 and the first general election to choose a prime minister and a cabinet.

In 1967, after the second election, in which the first black prime minister was elected, the Bahamas achieved full self-government. This meant that it administered its own internal affairs but was not fully sovereign or independent yet. The United Kingdom still retained control of foreign affairs, defense, and internal security. The Bahamas became fully independent on July 10, 1973, when its nominally adopted name of Commonwealth of the Bahama Islands was changed to Commonwealth of the Bahamas.

INTERNET LINKS

https://www.bbc.co.uk/news/world-latin-america-18723547
BBC offers a timeline of key events in the history of the Bahamas.

https://www.britannica.com/place/The-Bahamas
The online encyclopedia offers a good overview of Bahamian history.

https://www.smithsonianmag.com/history/last-days-blackbeard
Smithsonian magazine has a fascinating, in-depth article about the notorious Blackbeard.

https://www.smithsonianmag.com/smart-news/slave-revolt-ended -128-enslaved-people-free-bahamas
The story of the *Creole* slave revolt is presented on this site.

https://www.theguardian.com/news/2000/aug/28/ guardianobituaries1
This obituary of Lynden Pindling provides an overview of his controversial tenure as prime minister.

GOVERNMENT

A statue of Christopher Columbus stands on the stairway entrance to the Government House in Nassau, the capital of the Bahamas.

3

THE COMMONWEALTH OF THE Bahamas is a parliamentary democracy. It is an independent nation, but as a member of the Commonwealth of Nations, it exists under a constitutional monarchy. The Commonwealth is an association of fifty-three states that were previously part of the British Empire.

For 250 years, from 1723 to 1973, the Bahamas was a colony of the United Kingdom, and all the important decisions affecting the growth of the country and the welfare and taxation of the Bahamian people were made four thousand miles across the Atlantic Ocean, in London.

There was a brief period during the American Revolutionary War when the Bahamas fell to Spanish forces under General Bernardo de Gálvez in 1782. A British-American Loyalist expedition later recaptured the islands. The governors of the Bahamas enjoyed local authority after 1729, but until recently they were required to refer any major decisions to the British Colonial Office, and through that to the British Parliament.

As recently as the early 1950s, there were no political parties in the Bahamas, and Bahamians had no official body to express their concerns and wishes about the way the islands were governed. Twenty years later, however, the Bahamas had become a fully independent, sovereign country, with a government authorized by the electorate to decide on every aspect of government, including foreign relations and defense.

The flag of the Bahamas has three equal horizontal bands of aquamarine, gold, and aquamarine, with a black equilateral triangle on the hoist side. The gold represents the sun, or golden beaches, and the aquamarine represents the sea. The black represents the vigor and force of the Bahamian people, while the triangle symbolizes their enterprise and determination.

POLITICAL HISTORY

Lynden O. Pindling (*left*), premier of the Bahamas, attends the Bahamas Constitutional Conference in London in 1968. Seated next to him are Baron Ralph Grey (*center*), governor of Turks and Caicos Islands, and, Roland Symonette (*right*), leader of the United Bahamian Party.

Since long before World War II, the political assembly had been in the hands of a white oligarchy, a small group of powerful people who control a country. This group of merchants and lawyers were known as the Bay Street Boys. The term was derogatory, for this faction was blamed for practically everything that went wrong in the Bahamian economy. The Bay Street Boys dismissed the black residents as being politically irrelevant. But during the war, thousands of black soldiers lost their lives, a point that some African Bahamians drove home to their compatriots. This was the beginning of a shift in the political power base.

In 1953, a group led by Lynden O. Pindling founded the Progressive Liberal Party (PLP), with a political platform of improving the social, economic, and political situation in the Bahamas. The Bay Street Boys reacted by forming the United Bahamian Party (UBP) in 1958. Britain sent the secretary of state for the colonies to the Bahamas to determine the grassroots political sentiment, and as a result of his recommendations, the 1960s was a time of great political change in the Bahamas.

In 1964, a new Bahamian constitution was adopted, the first-ever specifically for the Bahamas itself. It replaced the colonial government structure with a two-chamber parliament elected by Bahamians and headed by a prime minister and a cabinet whose members were drawn from the political party with the most votes. The British Parliament continued to appoint a governor to look after British interests in the Bahamas, but now he acted only in consultation with the prime minister.

The UBP, led by Roland Symonette, won the first election by a narrow majority. The opposition in parliament, led by Lynden Pindling, adopted a political strategy of disobedience that climaxed in its boycott of parliament in 1967. This forced another election, and Pindling became the first black prime minister of the Bahamas.

He began the process of leading the country toward total independence from the United Kingdom. In 1969, changes to the constitution gave the Bahamas self-government, and only defense, foreign relations, and internal security remained in control of the British government.

Not all Bahamians wanted independence. Many felt there was no need to hurry the process, among them the Free National Movement (FNM), a 1971 coalition of the UBP and dissident members of the PLP. By majority vote, however, the electorate decided the issue when they elected Pindling for a second term in 1972.

Parliament Square is decorated in flags to celebrate Bahamian Independence Day.

A constitutional conference was called in London to discuss the proposal for complete independence. As a result of the London talks, a new constitution for the Bahamas was drawn up. At midnight on July 9, 1973, the birth of the independent nation of the Bahamas was symbolically recognized by the lowering of the Union Jack (the British flag) and the raising of the new Bahamian flag in Nassau.

LEADERSHIP CHANGES

Lynden Pindling was prime minister from 1967 until 1992, leading the Progressive Liberal Party. Toward the end of his last term in office, Bahamians were growing increasingly unhappy with his government's corrupt practices. Not surprisingly, the Free National Movement was voted into power in 1992, led by Hubert Alexander Ingraham. The FNM majority in 1992 was a slender 56 percent. The 1997 election saw a significant increase to 85 percent, for

Prime Minister Hubert Minnis of the Bahamas addresses the General Assembly of the United Nations in New York on September 28, 2018.

by then it was clear that the FNM's policies were helping the country recover after twenty-five years of mismanagement. In 2002, Ingraham lost to a resurgent PLP, under the leadership of his former law partner Perry Christie.

Christie and Ingraham repeatedly traded the premiership from 1992 to 2017. When Hubert Minnis was elected in 2017, he therefore became only the fourth prime minister in Bahamian history following independence. Minnis is a medical doctor trained in the United States, the United Kingdom, and the Caribbean.

THE CONSTITUTION

The 1973 constitution of the Commonwealth of the Bahamas proclaims the country to be a sovereign democratic state. It also establishes the executive, legislative, and judicial branches of government and creates the Public Service Commission, the Judicial and Legal Commission, and the Police Service Commission.

The constitution also guarantees fundamental rights and freedoms and the protection of these rights under the law without discrimination based on race, national origin, political opinion, color, creed, or gender. The constitution may be amended only by an act of parliament in combination with a popular referendum. It has been amended numerous times, most recently in 2016.

GOVERNMENT STRUCTURE

The Bahamas is a parliamentary democracy and a member of the Commonwealth of Nations, a group of countries once governed by the United Kingdom. As such, the Bahamas has retained the British monarch—at this writing, Queen Elizabeth II—as its head of state. She is represented by a Bahamian-born governor-general whom she appoints on the advice of

the prime minister of the Bahamas. In 2014, Dame Marguerite Pindling, the widow of the Bahamas' first prime minister, was appointed as the governor-general. This position is ceremonial.

The actual business of governing is conducted by the executive and legislative branches—the prime minister and the parliament.

The executive branch of government includes the prime minister as the head of government, and the cabinet, which has at least nine ministers, including the attorney general. The prime minister appoints the other cabinet members.

The parliament has two chambers—the Senate and the House of Assembly. The Senate has sixteen members who serve five-year terms. These

Queen Elizabeth II sits in a throne in the State Chamber in Nassau as she makes history opening the Bahamian Parliament for the first time in 1977.

members are appointed by the governor-general upon the advice of the prime minister and the opposition leader. The House of Assembly has thirty-nine seats. Members are directly elected by a simple majority vote by the citizenry, to serve five-year terms.

The constitution requires laws to be enacted by parliament in a certain manner—a bill is introduced in the House of Assembly, read three times, and debated. If it is passed, it becomes an act. The act is read three times in the Senate and then sent to the governor-general. When he or she has signed the act, it is published in the official journal of the government and becomes a law.

The Bahamas has a two-party system, and the voting age is eighteen. The next elections are to be held in May 2022.

THE JUSTICE SYSTEM

The justice system is modeled on the British common-law system but includes Bahamian statute law. Many members of the legal profession in the Bahamas have trained in and are eligible to practice in Britain. The judiciary is independent of government control.

The hierarchy of courts ranges from local magistrate's courts in New Providence and Grand Bahama to the Supreme Courts (one each in Nassau and Freeport) and the Court of Appeal. There is also the right of appeal to Her Majesty's Privy Council in England.

Appeals move upward; for example, an appeal from a decision of a Family Island commissioner is heard in a magistrate's court, while an appeal from a decision in a magistrate's court is heard in the Supreme Court. The attorney general and the Bahamas Bar Association constantly review the Bahamian justice system.

Two Royal Bahamas police officers stand on Bay Street in Nassau in 2014.

DEFENSE AND POLICE FORCES

The Bahamas has no army or navy. Its Royal Bahamas Defense Force performs mainly the duties of a coast guard service, which include the extremely difficult task of intercepting smugglers who operate in the waters surrounding the islands. The Royal Bahamas Police Force is responsible for the maintenance of law and order everywhere in the Bahamas.

INTERNET LINKS

http://www.bahamas.gov.bs/wps/portal/public/gov/government
This is the official site of the government of the Bahamas.

https://www.bbc.com/news/world-latin-america-18722984
The BBC country profile of the Bahamas provides a short section about the current prime minister.

https://www.cia.gov/library/publications/the-world-factbook/geos/bf.html
The CIA World Factbook provides up-to-date information on the Bahamian government.

https://www.loc.gov/law/help/guide/nations/bahamas.php
This US Library of Congress page provides many helpful links to sites regarding law and government in the Bahamas.

https://thenassauguardian.com/2012/07/16/the-bahamas-constitution-chapters-i-to-v.
This article provides an overview of important parts of the Bahamian constitution.

ECONOMY

A birds-eye view of the Bahama Islands highlights the white beaches and blue waters.

4

EVER SINCE THE ISLANDS' FIRST tourists arrived—Columbus and his crew in 1492—the beauty of the region has attracted visitors. Of course, Columbus wasn't a tourist in the modern sense; he was interested in something other than pretty scenery and a warm climate. But according to his journal, even he couldn't help but be impressed with the beauty of the place. He immediately claimed the land as Spain's own.

Determined to extract some economic profit from the islands, subsequent European settlers would quickly wreak disaster on the native population. If the Bahamian islands would not yield gold, then they would be made to grow crops, such as cotton and sugarcane. However, some of the islands, with their thin soils, were not well suited to such endeavors, despite the back-breaking work provided by unpaid labor—the enslaved workers. First these were the native islanders themselves, but when they died off from disease and unbearable working conditions, enslaved people from West Africa were imported.

Agriculture would never prove to be the islands' best bet, economically. Today, the sector accounts for just a tiny sliver of the nation's gross domestic product (GDP) and likewise employs a very small percent of the labor force.

Christopher Columbus said of the Bahamas, "The beauty of these islands surpasses that of any other and as much as the day surpasses the night in splendor." Not surprisingly, the Bahamas is a favorite tourist destination for Americans and Europeans.

A tour boat passes by the colorful houses in Nassau.

Instead, tourism has grown to be the major contributor, by far, to the Bahamian economy. But it wasn't always so. Tourism as an activity has been around for thousands of years, but until quite recently, it was a luxury only for the wealthy—and even then, mainly for health or religious purposes. It wasn't until the social changes of the Industrial Revolution brought about a sizable middle class of people with sufficient money and free time that leisure tourism became a concept. As hotels and restaurants were built to accommodate these new travelers, a whole new service industry developed.

And though many tourists come to the Bahamas on cruise ships, it was really with the advent of affordable air travel in the 1960s that mass tourism became a reality. Likewise, tourism in the Bahamas didn't surge until about the mid-twentieth century.

TOURISM TODAY

Tourism dominates the Bahamian economy. It accounts for almost 50 percent of GDP and directly or indirectly employs about half of the

> *Gross domestic product (GDP) is a measure of a country's total production. The number reflects the total value of goods and services produced over one year. Economists use it to determine whether a country's economy is growing or contracting. Growth is good, while a falling GDP means trouble. Dividing the GDP by the number of people in the country determines the GDP* per capita *(per person). This number provides an indication of a country's average standard of living—the higher the better.*
>
> *In 2017, the GDP per capita in the Bahamas was approximately $31,200. That rank is 65th out of 229 countries listed by the CIA World Factbook. (For comparison, the GDP per capita in the United States that year was $59,500 at number 19.)*

nation's labor force. Most visitors—90 percent—are from the United States and Canada. All major cruise lines operate services to the Bahamas. To extend the stay of passengers, the government allows ships to open their casinos and stores only if they remain in port for more than eighteen hours.

New Providence is the main tourist destination and has seen many hotel and casino developments, particularly in recent years. The largest resort on the island is the Baha Mar Resort on Cable Beach.

The Out Islands attract fewer visitors, but for vacationers looking for more off-the-beaten path locales, they offer quieter, more "authentic" experiences.

FINANCIAL SERVICES

The other major service-oriented economic activity in the Bahamas is banking and financial services, which accounts for about 15 percent of GDP. The Bahamas has been a well-known international tax haven for more than fifty years, and as a result, some of the world's wealthiest citizens have made their homes there. Among the country's attractions are its political stability, its generous tax laws (there is no tax in the Bahamas on income, profits, or inheritance), and the ease with which people can reinvest their money. Many foreign banks have been attracted to the Bahamas for the same

With great expectations and much fanfare, the Bahama's largest and grandest resort, the Baha Mar, was scheduled to open in May 2015. The three-hotel resort—with

forty-two restaurants and lounges, a 100,000-square-foot (92,903-square-meter) casino, 0.5 miles (0.8 km) of beachfront, eleven swimming pools, a world-class golf course, a spa, and more—was heralded as the new top spot among Bahamian resorts, and one of the biggest in North America.

And then, at the last minute, it didn't open. Instead, the nearly-finished resort declared bankruptcy. Some two thousand employees, ready to go, were suddenly out of jobs. Bitter legal battles ensued between the contractor and the construction company. Finally, the Hong Kong-based conglomerate Chow Tai Fook Enterprises agreed to buy the resort from the previous owner, Export-Import Bank of China, for an undisclosed sum.

The resort finally opened, in stages, starting in April 2017. A year later, the $4 billion project was fully operational, and expected to generate some 12 percent of the Bahamas' GDP.

reason; Bay Street in the center of downtown Nassau has one of the largest concentrations of international banks in the world, giving it the nickname Little Switzerland.

In December 2000, partly as a response to appearing on the Financial Action Task Force blacklist of Non-Cooperative Countries or Territories (NCCTs)—that is, countries perceived to be noncooperative in the global fight against money laundering and terrorist financing—the Bahamas enacted a legislative package to better regulate the financial sector. This included the creation of the Financial Intelligence Unit and enforcement of "know your customer" rules. Other initiatives included the enactment of the Foundations Act in 2004 and the planned introduction of legislation to regulate private trust companies. Many international businesses have left the Bahamas in response to these new rules.

MANUFACTURING

Despite government incentives to boost manufacturing and agriculture, those sectors combined contribute only about 10 percent of GDP and show little growth.

Government infrastructure projects and private construction provide the main industrial activity. The only shipyard in the Bahamas is in Freeport, and it specializes in the repair of passenger and cruise ships. There is limited production of minerals. Sand is dredged off the banks and used for limestone and the production of commercial sand, which supply the local construction industry. There is also limited production of sea salt for export to the United States. Pharmaceutical company PFC Bahamas produces a small quantity of products for export, and the Bahamas Oil Refining Company (BORCO) has a refinery on the islands, but these are individual enterprises and do not represent any large industrial presence. There is a substantial brewing industry. Companies such as Bacardi distill rum and other spirits on the islands, while international breweries such as Commonwealth Brewery produce beers including the Heineken, Guinness, and Kalik brands.

Evaporation fields harvest salt from the sea on Great Inagua Island.

AGRICULTURE AND FISHERIES

Agriculture accounts for 2.3 percent of GDP. The Bahamas exports lobster and some fish but does not raise these items commercially. There is no large-scale agriculture, and most agricultural products are consumed domestically.

The Bahamas imports about $250 million in food each year, representing about 80 percent of its food consumption. The Out Islands rely on foodstuffs to be delivered from Nassau on government barges about once or twice a week, which can add to the price of food.

The government aims to expand food production to reduce imports and generate foreign exchange. It actively seeks foreign investment aimed at increasing agricultural exports, particularly specialty food items. The government officially lists beef and pork production and processing, fruits and nuts, dairy production, winter vegetables, and mariculture (shrimp farming) as the areas in which it wishes to encourage foreign investment.

TRADE

The Bahamas' main exports are rock lobsters, mineral products, salt, rum, chemicals, and fruits and vegetables. Major imports are machinery and transport equipment, manufactured goods, chemicals, mineral fuels, food, and live animals. The country's most important trading partner is the United States.

Shipping containers are ready to be offloaded in the port of Freeport on Grand Bahama Island.

The Bahamas is a member of the Caribbean Community (CARICOM), an organization of twenty Caribbean nations and dependencies. CARICOM's main purposes are to promote economic integration and cooperation among its members, to ensure that the benefits of integration are equitably shared, and to coordinate foreign policy.

US president Barack Obama (*left*) speaks as Bahamas prime minister Perry Christie looks on during a meeting with Caribbean Community (CARICOM) leaders at the University of the West Indies in 2015 in Kingston, Jamaica.

TRANSPORTATION

The country's international airports are in Chub Cay, Rock Sound, Great Exuma Island, Freeport, and Nassau. Bahamasair, the national airline, is headquartered in Nassau and provides flights to these airports from adjacent countries as well as domestic service to other smaller airports or airstrips on the islands. Most people entering the Bahamas do so via Miami, Florida. The main seaports are Nassau on New Providence and Freeport on Grand Bahama.

The major islands have a good system of roads. Driving is on the left side of the road, unlike in America and Continental Europe. Most of the major islands have a bus service, and minibuses called jitneys travel to the main settlements. Several people traveling in the same general direction often share taxis, which are plentiful. Taxis come in many shapes and sizes, from compact cars to minivans and even limousines.

As the Bahamas is an island nation, transportation by boat is important. Twice a week, mail boats leave Potter's Cay Dock in Nassau and head toward the smaller Family (Out) Islands. Mail boats used to carry mail, but today their primary function in the Bahamas is to carry cargo, which can be anything from livestock to dry goods. Mail boats tend to be somewhat older boats and are often brightly painted to reflect the colorful influence of the island

culture, making them a good choice for travelers interested in an authentic island experience. Other boat travel options include ferries and yachts, and visitors can even charter their own boats.

Transport of a different nature involves drug smuggling. The Bahamas is located between cocaine and marijuana producers in South America and drug consumers in the United States and Europe. As such, it has been a main transshipment point and an offshore financial center for these illicit industries.

TELECOMMUNICATION

The telecommunications system in the Bahamas is totally automatic and highly developed. The Bahamas Domestic Submarine Network, a fiber optic cable system, links twenty of the islands and is designed to satisfy increasing demand for voice and broadband Internet services. About 80 percent of the population are Internet users. Most people rely on cellular phone service, though the land lines are in good condition and also in use.

INTERNET LINKS

http://www.bahamas.gov.bs
The government portal of the Bahamas includes information on business and finance.

https://www.bloomberg.com/news/articles/2018-05-10/baha-mar -bahamas-resort-review
This Bloomberg article reviews the opening of the Baha Mar resort.

https://borgenproject.org/poverty-in-the-bahamas
This organization offers information about poverty in the Bahamas.

https://www.cia.gov/library/publications/the-world-factbook/ geos/bf.html
The CIA World Factbook includes up-to-date information on the Bahamian economy.

https://www.myoutislands.com/bahamas-map
Tourism possibilities offered in the Out Islands are presented on this site.

http://www.tourismtoday.com/services/statistics
This site provides tourism statistics for the Bahamas.

https://www.wttc.org/-/media/files/reports/economic-impact -research/countries-2017/bahamas2017.pdf
This 2017 PDF report from the World Travel and Tourism Council has in-depth information about how tourism affects the Bahamian economy.

ENVIRONMENT

The bright coral-pink flamingos of the Bahamas are not only national symbols but popular tourist attractions.

5

THE BAHAMAS' ENVIRONMENT IS its fortune, as its main industry is tourism, and the number of tourists who visit each year is more than four times the population of the islands. Tourists are attracted to the Bahamas because of its abundant wildlife and pristine beaches.

The Bahamas is home to some of the healthiest reef systems and greatest marine biodiversity in the Caribbean. Citizens, residents, and developers all have an opportunity and responsibility to play a critical role in preserving these resources.

The West Indian flamingo, also known as the American flamingo, is the national bird of the Bahamas. Along with the blue marlin, the national fish, it is pictured in the country's coat of arms.

Caribbean reef sharks swim off the shores of the islands.

ANIMALS IN THE BAHAMAS

A leaf-nosed bat.

The archipelago has only thirteen native land mammal species, all of which are endangered. Twelve of them are bats; the most common mammal in the Bahamas is the leaf-nosed bat. The other native terrestrial mammal is the hutia, a cat-sized brown rodent akin to a guinea pig. Wild boars roam the backcountry of some of the larger islands. Feral cattle, donkeys, and horses, descendants of animals released after the demise of the salt industry, outnumber humans on some of the southern islands.

The Bahamas has plenty of slithery things, including forty-four species of reptiles. The country's symbol could well be the curly-tailed lizard, a critter found throughout most of the islands and easily spotted sunning on rocks, its tail coiled like a spring over its back. Humpback and blue whales are often sighted in the waters east of the islands. Atlantic bottlenose dolphins frequent these waters, as do the less-often-seen spotted dolphins.

PROTECTING WILDLIFE

The Bahamas is a member of the Convention on International Trade in Endangered Species of Wild Flora and Fauna (CITES), which was created in 1973 to protect wildlife against exploitation of species on a scale that threatens its existence. In accordance with CITES rules, the Bahamas has divided its endangered species into two groups: those near extinction and those likely to become endangered. No trade is allowed in the first category, while limited trade is permitted for the second.

Among the species nearing extinction are peregrine falcons, Bahama parrots, four species of turtles (loggerhead, hawksbill, green, and leatherback turtles), Bahamian rock iguanas, American crocodiles, whales, dolphins, and West Indian manatees.

THE SWIMMING PIGS OF EXUMA

What could be cuter than pigs swimming in the ocean on a beautiful sandy beach? On Big Major Cay of the Exuma Islands, a small colony of about twenty feral pigs has been doing exactly that for several decades, much to the delight of tourists.

No one is sure how the pigs came to live on this otherwise uninhabited (by humans) island. They are not native to the region. Local lore suggests the original animals were survivors of a shipwreck, or perhaps left there by sailors who planned to return to eat them—but never did. In any case, the animals adapted well to their environment. They foraged in the woods and found fresh water there, and, like some dogs, evidently enjoyed swimming in the shallow ocean waters.

Today, they are a famous tourist attraction, and the cay is nicknamed Pig Island. The friendly piggies aren't shy and often run—or swim—up to visiting tourists, snorting their greetings. Several boat tours stop by every day.

It was all just adorable until February 2017, when nearly half the pigs were found dead. At first, rumors claimed that tourists had fed the pigs alcohol, but the cause was eventually determined to be sand ingestion. The seven or more dead pigs were found to have a lot of sand in their stomachs. That didn't let tourists off the hook, however.

Animal welfare officials surmise that tourists were leaving so much food behind on the beach that the pigs no longer needed to forage in the woods. Instead, they stayed on the beach and ate discarded human snacks, often half buried in sand. After the deaths, the beaches were cleaned and the government was reconsidering allowing tourists to interact freely with the animals.

The Ministry of Agriculture is the CITES managing authority in the Bahamas, while the Bahamas National Trust acts as the scientific authority. Together these organizations grant permits for trade in endangered species and educate people on the need to preserve wildlife, particularly endangered species.

NATIONAL PARKS AND RESERVES

The Bahamas national park system protects the world's largest breeding colony of West Indian flamingos, one of the world's longest underwater cave systems, a critically important sea turtle research facility, and one of the most successful marine fishery reserves in the Caribbean. In 2002 the park system was doubled in size, an unprecedented accomplishment in protected-area history. Ten new national parks were created, protecting both marine and terrestrial territories, bringing the total protected area under the system to more than 2 million acres (809,371 hectares).

CONSERVATION ORGANIZATIONS

The Bahamas has myriad conservation organizations, both governmental and nongovernmental, to protect the environment. The Department of Agriculture in the Bahamas is responsible for the conservation and enforcement of wildlife laws, such as stopping illegal trade in the Bahama parrot, which is a very popular pet worldwide. The forestry department of the Bahamas government manages what little is left of the Bahamian forests.

The Bahamas Reef Environment Educational Foundation (BREEF) was founded in 1993 by Sir Nicholas Nuttall to address growing concerns about the state of the Bahamas's marine environments. BREEF is a nonprofit organization dedicated to protecting the Bahamian marine environment through education.

The Bahamas Environment, Science, and Technology (BEST) Commission was established in 1994 to better manage the difficult implementation of

A view of trees in Lucaya National Park on Grand Bahama Island.

multilateral environment agreements. It also reviews all environmental impact assessments and environmental management plans for development projects carried out within the Bahamas.

The Bahamas National Trust came into being due to an effort to save the West Indian flamingo and to create the world's first land and sea park. Today it has evolved into a statutory, nonprofit, nongovernmental organization devoted to the conservation and management of the country's natural and historic resources.

CORAL REEFS

The coral reefs provide Bahamians with food. The nooks and crannies found between the various reefs are safe houses for an abundance of marine life ranging from spiny lobsters to yellowtail snappers. Coral reefs also provide the Bahamas with storm security, which is priceless. The growth pattern of reefs is such that they put themselves at the mercy of an oncoming wave and are the first to take the brunt of the storm, thereby decreasing the size of the incoming surge. A third benefit of the reefs is their boost to the Bahamian economy, in that their beauty and the marine life they house attract tourists from all over the world.

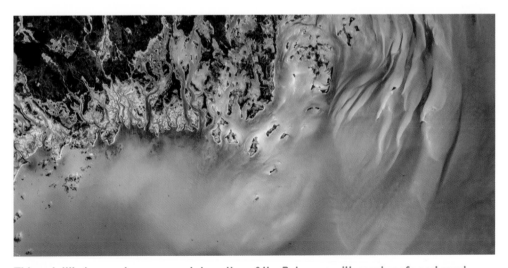

This satellite image shows a coastal section of the Bahamas with coral reefs and sand structures visible.

Overfishing has caused a drastic decline in the supply of conch throughout the Caribbean. During the past few decades, intense fishing pressure has led to the collapse of the conch fishery in many Caribbean countries.

The Bahamian conch fishery is slowly becoming depleted. Fishermen have to go farther to find conch, as the near-shore supply is drying up. In the Bahamas, it's illegal to catch immature conch, but a large proportion of the conch catch are juvenile conch that have not had a chance to reproduce.

In some parts of the northern Bahamas, up to 90 percent of the conch landed are juveniles. Students in South Eleuthera studied old and new piles of conch shells. They found that in the piles at least ten years old, 5 percent of the conch were juveniles, while of the conch caught today, 95 percent are juveniles.

Catching conch before they have reproduced threatens the sustainability of this resource and the livelihoods of the fishermen who depend on it. The conch is listed as a threatened species by CITES. To reverse this, stronger enforcement of the Bahamian laws regarding harvesting conch is needed, and a network of marine reserves where no conch fishing is allowed must be put in place as quickly as possible, to allow conch to breed and the population to recover.

The reefs are under threat from a number of sources. Improper fishing methods are causing serious damage to the coral reefs and the animals that live there. Some fishermen use bleach and detergent to drive lobsters from their dens, but this has destroyed coral reefs and reduced lobster numbers. Oil seriously damages the reefs by killing the coral polyps that create them. Run-off of fertilizers into the ocean leads to increased growth of algae that can overrun the corals. Algal and bacterial blooms resulting from these excess nutrients can cause fish to die in large numbers. Excessive sedimentation from coastal development projects that seep into the ecosystems also create havoc by smothering corals and damaging the creeks and wetlands that serve as nursery habitats for commercially important species of fish.

POLLUTION

Pollution continues to be one of the main challenges the Bahamas faces in maintaining its environment. A number of laws are in place to protect the environment, but given the sprawling nature of the islands, enforcement is a challenge. Problems associated with marine, coastal, air, and land pollution could have long-lasting negative impacts on the environment if left unchecked. Major causes of pollution in coastal areas of the Bahamas include leaks and spills of petrochemicals; run-offs from land pollutants, including fertilizers and pesticides used in agriculture and landscaping; run-off of sediment from coastal development; seepage of sewage from septic tanks; and the improper disposal of garbage such as cans, bottles, plastic bags, and other household waste.

Trash left by tourists piles up on a beach on Paradise Island.

DUMPING The indiscriminate littering of plastic bags and other materials on beaches and in the ocean continues to have a devastating impact on marine life. For instance, turtles and other creatures mistake plastic bags for jellyfish. In addition, the dumping of materials such as heavy metals and lead compounds contributes to toxic air pollutants that can be harmful to human beings. The dumping of automobiles and consumer goods such as refrigerators throughout the islands is contributing to land pollution.

AIR POLLUTION Another major source of pollution in the Bahamas is carbon monoxide emissions from cars, trucks, and buses. These emissions are higher when vehicles are not properly maintained. Carbon monoxide makes it difficult for body parts to get the oxygen necessary to function at their optimum. Overexposure to carbon monoxide can result in dizziness, fatigue, and headaches.

PESTICIDES The use of pesticides is also a major concern. In a marine environment, pesticides can kill important ecosystems and disrupt food webs. Pesticides can also present a number of health challenges to human beings, particularly if they enter freshwater systems and contaminate drinking water.

WASTE TREATMENT AND DISPOSAL

The Bahamas, like most other developing countries, is grappling with a tremendous waste problem. The Bahamas produces more than 300,000 tons (272,155 metric tons) of waste annually, and a sustainable solution has not yet been instituted. Landfills in the Bahamas regularly catch fire because as waste decomposes, it produces large amounts of gas that burns uncontrollably beneath the surface if it is not collected or vented. The large, engineered Bahamas Landfill on New Providence Island was never completed according to specifications and accordingly fails to function adequately. Fires are common, which pollute the air, and seepage pollutes the underground water table.

In 2015, the first state-of-the-art recycling facility was opened on the island, but there is as yet no national policy on recycling. Private initiatives try to fill that gap.

Meanwhile, as officials try to figure out a solution to the failing urban landfill situation, the problem of waste disposal on the other Bahamian islands lags behind. On many of the Family (Out) Islands, a long tradition of open-air dumps—dumping wrecked vehicles, large appliances, and other waste materials in natural landscapes—has blighted many parts of the beautiful country. Romauld Ferreira, the minister of the environment, said in 2018, "We must stop this 'dumping in the bush' culture." He expressed the hope that landfill upgrades, and improved education, would help to change people's behavior and thinking about environmental stewardship. Each island needs its own dynamic waste management solutions, he said.

INTERNET LINKS

http://www.agrra.org/front-page-news/bahamas-coral-reefs
The Atlantic and Gulf Rapid Reef Assessment provides a PDF of the 2016 report "Bahamas Coral Reef Report Card."

https://bnt.bs
The Bahamas National Trust has information about the country's parks, ecosystems, and animals.

https://www.fodors.com/world/caribbean/bahamas/experiences/ news/photos/10-animals-to-meet-in-the-bahamas
This travel site offers a slide show of animals in the Bahamas.

https://news.nationalgeographic.com/2017/03/swimming-pigs -bahamas-death
This article examines the reasons behind the 2017 deaths of the famous swimming pigs.

https://www.nature.org/ourinitiatives/regions/caribbean/ bahamas/index.htm
The Nature Conservancy site discusses environmental issues in the Bahamas.

https://news.mongabay.com/2018/02/queen-conch-dying-out-in -the-bahamas-despite-marine-parks
This article looks at the collapse of the conch population in the Bahamas.

BAHAMIANS

A family plays hide and seek in Nassau.

6

In 2017, there were about 330,000 to 350,000 people living in the Bahamas. About two-thirds of the population live on New Providence Island (where Nassau is located), and about half of the remaining one-third live on Grand Bahama (the location of Freeport). The others are scattered throughout the remaining inhabited islands.

WHO ARE THE BAHAMIANS? Today's residents carry the history of the archipelago in their blood. The original islanders, the Lucayans, disappeared several centuries ago. Their population was so completely annihilated that no descendants remain.

Many Bahamian families trace their ancestry back to the colonizing Eleutheran Adventurers who came with Captain William Sayle, seeking religious freedom by settling on the island of Eleuthera in 1647; to the Loyalists who migrated to the Bahamas after the Revolutionary War; and to the American Southerners who came just before and during the American Civil War. Many of these people brought their slaves, who eventually made up the majority of the Bahamian population. There are also Bahamians who claim as ancestors some of the more notorious pirates who once made the Bahamas their home.

AFRICAN BAHAMIANS

According to the Bahamas' 2010 census, 92.7 percent of the country's people identify as African (90.6 percent) or African/European mixed (2.1 percent). These African Bahamians, or Afro-Bahamians, are at least partly descended from people who came directly or indirectly from Africa, mostly as enslaved laborers. The majority of those people came from Western and Central African regions, including Senegal, Burkina Faso, Nigeria, Ghana, and Cameroon.

An African Bahamian woman shares a hug with her son.

Many were enslaved people who migrated with their Loyalist owners in the early 1800s, after the American Revolution, to work the plantations on the islands. Ultimately the plantations failed. Not long after, in 1834, slavery was abolished throughout the British Empire, which included the Bahamas. The practice continued in the United States, however, and as the British Royal Navy intercepted slave ships bound for America, the people aboard were freed and resettled in the Bahamas. Some seven thousand Africans came to the islands in this way. The descendants of those people, slave or free, stayed on in the Bahamas to become the backbone of its citizenry.

Friendliness and warmth toward perfect strangers are characteristics of most African Bahamians. Any human population includes a mix of very different personalities, of course, but in broad general terms, African Bahamians are said to love a good conversation. It is not unusual to walk down the street in a Bahamian town, fall into earnest conversation with

Bahamians trace their roots by their names. When African people were captured, enslaved, and shipped to the "New World," their names and languages were also taken from them. Instead, the people were given European names, often the last name of their owners. The last name Rolle, for example, is common on Great Exuma Island. The ancestors of today's Rolles took their name from Lord John Rolle, a wealthy British planter who gave his land to his former slaves after emancipation. Other common last names include Albury, Higgs, Johnson, Knowles, Smith, and Symonette.

Having lost the family names that originated in Africa long made it impossible for the descendants of enslaved people—in the Bahamas and throughout the Americas—to trace their heritage. Today, DNA analysis offers an opportunity to right that old wrong. The Bahamas DNA Project, launched in 2004, collects genealogy information supported by genetic information to help Bahamians trace their ancestry.

a total stranger, and become fast friends very quickly. By the same token, Bahamians are usually very helpful people. If they see people who are clearly not local wandering around as though lost and in need of help, they will quickly offer them directions, advice, and a bit of friendly conversation.

The gregariousness of African Bahamians is evident in their large and extended families. Bahamian family gatherings, which take place during most public holidays, might well include grandparents, parents, children, and first, second, and even third and fourth cousins. Often all that is needed to be included in a family gathering is a common origin, such as having been born on the same island. Common interests, such as enjoyment of similar food and conversation, also give Bahamians the right to membership in a "family" group.

"Laid-back" is said to be another characteristic typical of many African Bahamians. This is perhaps more a description of the culture than of the individuals themselves. This relaxed approach to life leads to humorous satire about procrastination and losing track of time, but it's largely a matter of enjoying life in a beautiful place.

EUROPEAN BAHAMIANS

White Bahamians make up about 4.7 percent of the population. For the most part, they or their ancestors came from Britain or the United States. Often they are better educated than their African counterparts, hold better jobs, and own finer houses.

CONCHY JOES "Conchy Joe" (KONK-ee JO) is a (frequently disparaging) slang term applied to anyone of European descent, especially those whose families have been in the Bahamas for as long as anyone can remember. Countless Conchy Joe families are now racially mixed, but the typical Conchy Joe is white, with blue eyes and blonde hair. Conchy Joes tend to stand out through their display of ostentatious possessions and behavior. In a disparaging sense, the term is also sometimes applied to a Bahamian of mixed race who "acts white."

HAITIANS

A large number of Haitian migrants live in the Bahamas. In the big cities, they form much of the manual-labor force. The number of Haitians in the country is unclear, since many are undocumented and were not included in the 2010 census. Some 10 to 25 percent of the Bahamian population is thought to be people of Haitian descent. In 2014, the International Organization for Migration estimated the number of Haitians in the Bahamas at nearly seventy thousand people (18 percent of the population), with between twenty thousand and fifty thousand of them being undocumented.

In the Bahamas, the presence of this large population is openly referred to as the "Haitian problem." Whereas the Bahamas is the wealthiest of the

Caribbean nations, Haiti is just the opposite. In fact, it is the poorest country in the Western Hemisphere, and after the catastrophic earthquake of 2010, the situation there is all the more dire. It's not surprising, therefore, that many Haitians have tried to find a better life in neighboring countries, including the Bahamas. Large numbers have arrived illegally, however, and that presents a problem—according to the Bahamian government. Many Bahamians are openly hostile to the Haitians and believe they are a burden to society and a drag on the country's limited resources.

Haitians, who tend to be shorter and darker-skinned than most Bahamians, are mainly French Creole speakers and live in communities of their own, usually in the very poorest neighborhoods. Most members of this migrant population have not received much education. Both European and African Bahamians tend to look down on them, and some resent the Haitians for "stealing" jobs—even though most of these jobs (such as gardening, domestic work, and cleaning) are not ones that the Bahamians want for themselves.

In October 2017, Prime Minister Hubert Minnis caused a stir when he announced that all "irregular" (unauthorized) migrants of all nationalities should voluntarily return to their country of origin by the end of that calendar year or face arrest and deportation. And indeed, thousands of people have been deported. Some of the Haitians in question were born in the Bahamas and have never set foot in Haiti. However, the Bahamian government does not recognize citizenship as a birthright. Since 2014, citizenship is conferred automatically to those who are

- born in the Bahamas to married parents, with either parent being a Bahamian citizen;
- born to an unmarried Bahamian female in or outside of the Bahamas;
- born outside of the Bahamas to a married Bahamian male who was not born outside the Bahamas;
- adopted by a married Bahamian male; or
- adopted by a single Bahamian female.

All other residents desiring citizenship, including those born in the country to non-Bahamian parents, are required to apply for it between the ages of eighteen and nineteen. The process, however, requires a long list of documents—such as parents' birth certificates or passports—that the Haitians often lack. These rules have essentially created an impoverished underclass of stateless people.

MINORITIES

Chinese, Hispanics, Greeks, and Jews make up about 3 percent of the population. Many of them arrived in the early twentieth century from the United States, Hong Kong, and the surrounding islands. They tend to interact within their own communities rather than with other Bahamians.

BAHAMIAN DRESS

The proximity of the Bahamas to the United States means that American influence is very strong on the islands. There is little difference between the attitude to fashion in Miami and in Nassau, except perhaps for a certain island flair.

Designer clothes are all the rage in the Bahamas, despite their high cost due to import taxes, and these are what Bahamians wear on the street—the flashier the better. Bahamians have a very exuberant color sense, and this is reflected in the combination of clothes they wear. They also apply their taste for vivid colors to their houses, which can be painted in every known shade.

As religion is a very important aspect of Bahamian life, most Bahamians possess an extensive Sunday wardrobe of church clothes. The hats worn by women are particularly important items of church attire, and proper shoes must be worn by all, with socks or stockings.

Many Bahamians also have a good knowledge of and interest in the ceremonial dress worn by their African ancestors, including the Ibo, Mandingo, Yoruba, and Congo tribes. They very rarely wear African-style clothing, however, except on very special occasions.

Hairstyles are important to Bahamians, especially the women. No amount of attention to grooming, braiding, perming, straightening, or tinting is too much if it means achieving just the right result.

PEOPLE-TO-PEOPLE

One of the best ways for visitors to get to know the Bahamas and Bahamians is through the government-sponsored People-to-People program. Through this program, run by the Ministry of Tourism, tourists and visiting businesspeople are matched by age, interests, and profession with Bahamian individuals or families and spend some time in their company during their stay on the islands. This contact can be as simple as having a meal together or as involved as spending several days learning about the country and its attractions. Because Bahamians tend to be friendly and outgoing, this opportunity to understand them in their own environment often results in long-term friendship. Currently about five hundred Bahamians participate in the People-to-People program.

As part of the program, the People-to-People coordinator organizes a monthly tea party hosted by the governor-general's wife at Government House, the residence of the governor-general. Related programs target foreign students studying in Bahamian colleges, pen pals, and the spouses of delegates attending conferences.

INTERNET LINKS

https://www.cia.gov/library/publications/the-world-factbook/geos/bf.html
The CIA World Factbook has statistics on "People and Society" in the Bahamas.

http://www.noellenicolls.com/so-called-haitian-problem-bahamas-big-lie-cultural-attitudes
A Bahamian civil rights activist provides her take on the so-called "Haitian Problem."

LIFESTYLE

A woman weaves a traditional basket on Cat Island in the Bahamas.

7

E VERYDAY LIFE IN THE BAHAMAS IS relaxing and laid back. At least, that's certainly the image the tourism sector tries to broadcast. Of course, not everyone in the Bahamas is on vacation—work as well as family life can require times of hard, focused concentration and effort.

That said, there is an aspect of the culture that emphasizes enjoying life. There can be very little sense of urgency in the Bahamas, and the general attitude about time reflects this. Although events that are scheduled to happen at a particular time usually do (store opening

Bahamians are generally relaxed and easygoing folks with an engaging sense of humor and an elastic sense of time—they call it BT, or Bahamian Time.

A man and his son work their conch stand at the Port Lucaya Marketplace in Freeport.

hours, for instance), other indicated times may be merely approximate, especially outside the major cities. Taking a dinner invitation for 7:30 p.m. literally, for example, could cause a guest to arrive at least an hour before the host is ready to receive anyone. When a mail boat captain announces that his boat will depart at 10 p.m., it probably will leave sometime that night when everything has been loaded, but the chances of its leaving exactly at 10 p.m. are slight.

URBAN VERSUS RURAL

The Bahamian islands have varying settlement patterns and degrees of development. The infrastructure—roads, housing, and even golf courses—of any island usually depends on investment by development companies that reap profits from sales of houses and condominiums to foreigners and vacationers. San Salvador, for example, one of the Family Islands, enjoyed several periods of development—first in the 1930s, when the entrepreneur Harry Oakes built a hotel (it failed); then in the 1950s and 1960s, when the US Navy (using the hotel building as a base) ran a submarine and missile tracking operation; then from the late 1970s onward, when home and leisure developers realized the potential of the island for residents and vacationers. A Club Med opened there in 1992.

About 83 percent of Bahamians live in urban areas, where the pace of life is a little faster than in the rural areas. In the countryside, including many of the Family Islands, the rhythm of life often proceeds at much the same pace as it always has—in harmony with the seasons and the hours of daylight and darkness. Whereas urban dwellers tend to live in orderly communities characterized by a logical system of addresses and some uniformity in housing styles, home to a rural Bahamian can mean almost anything from a newly constructed brick house to a tin shack, and these are not necessarily built along a named road.

Bahamians are generally proud of where they live and of their community, often using it as part of their identity when describing themselves. They have no natural preference for town living, and many urban Bahamians confess to envying those who live less hectic lives on the less inhabited islands.

The pastel-colored houses of Nassau glow in the sunlight.

HOUSING

The majority of Bahamians live in small houses, but what they lack in size, they more than make up for in color. It is not unusual to see an orange house with a purple interior, for instance, or grand ornamentation inside and outside the house.

There are some architecturally outstanding homes in the Bahamas, particularly in Nassau and Freeport, many of them in quite exclusive residential districts. These houses were built in the characteristic "island" style, with covered porches, shaded balconies all around, sundecks or gables, shuttered windows, and several doors. The interiors are graciously decorated. Outdoors they typically have a lush garden, carefully landscaped and tended. In old Loyalist settlements, there are still old mansions and houses in the New England style.

Whatever the size, style, or color of their house, Bahamians are very house-proud and hospitable. An invitation to a meal or simply to "set awhile" and talk is not uncommon.

THE ROLE OF THE FAMILY

Bahamians have a strong, fundamental belief in the value of the family. Many Bahamians come from quite large families. This is especially true of the black Bahamian community, where extended families that include cousins many times removed support each other financially as well as in finding work and negotiating settlements whenever family differences threaten to disrupt the peace and stability of the group.

Bahamians have great respect for their elders. Grandfathers and grandmothers often continue to live with one of their children and are important influences in the raising of their grandchildren. It is more common than it used to be for both parents to work outside the home, making the role of the grandparents even more important.

The traditional roles of parents in a Western country are the norm in the Bahamas. The father is the head of the

A farmer on Great Exuma Island holds his baby granddaughter.

family and the disciplinarian, while the mother concerns herself more with the domestic needs of the family—cooking, housecleaning, doing laundry, and looking after the children's welfare—even if she also works outside the home. Grown children usually continue to live at home until they have completed their education and often until they marry.

BAHAMIAN WOMEN

In the old days, women tended to stay at home and take care of the children. However, with increased education, changing attitudes, and the development of the tourism industry, most women now work outside the home—many in leadership positions. In 2018, for example, the Bahamian parliament had a total of twelve female members in both the Senate and the House of Assembly. That relatively small number placed the nation at number 142 of 190 countries. (For comparison, that same year, the United States was ranked 103rd and the United Kingdom ranked 39th.)

While the government respects the rights of women, the constitution and the law discriminate against them. Unlike men, women cannot confer Bahamian citizenship to foreign-born spouses. The Bahamas remains one of only two countries in the Western Hemisphere that denies mothers the right to confer nationality to their children on an equal basis with men. Another example of unequal treatment is seen in inheritance law. Where no will exists, possessions of the dead pass to the oldest living male relative.

Violence against women is a serious problem. A private, government-aided crisis center runs a public awareness campaign on domestic violence, and a domestic court presides over family matters such as legal separation, maintenance payments, and court orders to protect women against abusive partners. The government provides a toll-free hotline with trained counselors for each inhabited island. These volunteers counsel women suffering from abuse at home.

A Bahamian woman and her daughter smile while they work at their food stall at New Bight Beach on Cat Island.

However, women's-rights groups have cited a general reluctance on the part of law enforcement authorities in the Bahamas to intervene in domestic disputes.

COMING INTO THE WORLD

Many Bahamians are staunch Christians, so the Bahamian life cycle tends to be dominated by the customs of the church. Baptists make up the largest Christian denomination, followed by Anglicans, Catholics, Methodists, and Seventh-Day Adventists.

At the same time, the African heritage of many Bahamians is still evident. For instance, a new child will almost always be christened in a formal ceremony in church with all the family in attendance. Godparents are often appointed to look after the child's spiritual welfare in the years to come.

Before then, however, a black cord is likely to have been tied around the newborn's wrist to guard against the entry of evil spirits into the unchristened body, and a Bible might have been placed at the head of the crib to strengthen this protection. A traditionally superstitious new mother also carefully avoids walking over "grave dirt," or it may take her a long time to recover from the effects of childbirth! In the Bahamas, a christening is a good excuse for a party and a gathering with the extended family.

THE WEDDING

Weddings in the Bahamas have taken place under almost all imaginable circumstances. The knot can be tied in conventional fashion in a historic church, under palm trees on one of a few thousand deserted tropical islands, in a privately chartered yacht, or even underwater with scuba gear. The more exotic weddings, however, are for the tourists. At the marriage registrar's discretion, a couple needs to be in the Bahamas for as little as three days before they can be married there, though in normal circumstances the period of residence is fifteen days.

The true Bahamian is likely to be traditional. "Pomp and circumstance" best describes the Bahamian wedding. Money is almost no object for any Bahamian bride; this is her day, and everyone must be reminded of it. The designs of the bride's and bridesmaids' gowns are extremely important, and no effort is spared to make the bridal entourage as spectacular as possible.

During the ceremony, music plays an important part (as it does in all other Bahamian celebrations), and the wedding march will almost always be heard in a church. After the ceremony, the reception is as lavish as the bride's parents can afford, complete with music and entertainment, speeches, and the ritual throwing of the bridal bouquet into the crowd on the couple's departure.

THE FUNERAL

If a wedding is an important social event, a funeral is no less so. The death of a loved one is naturally a sad occasion, but true Bahamians go out of their way to make the sendoff for relatives and friends memorable. Obituaries published in the newspapers describe the deceased in glowing terms and invite all acquaintances to pay their respects. They can attend the wake, an occasion for all who knew the deceased to gather and talk about his or her life, from time to time refreshing themselves with generous amounts of food and drink. Wakes often begin in the evening and last all night, ending with a service conducted in church. Then the coffin is carried in a procession to the cemetery, to the accompaniment of music, perhaps from a brass band. The usual form is an outward show of grief through tears and the singing of dirges. Long after a loved one has gone, parties may be held to mark the anniversary of his or her death.

EDUCATION

Up until the mid-nineteenth century, education in the Bahamas was provided to the children of well-to-do white families and only selectively to academically able nonwhites, mainly through church-funded schools. Those who could afford an overseas education sent their children to schools in the United States, Canada, and Britain. Public education from the late nineteenth to the early twentieth century was provided by Christian missionary schools.

Today school attendance is universal throughout the Bahamas. There are more than two hundred schools, the majority of which are funded and run by the government through the Ministry of Education. They coexist with private schools founded by various religious orders.

The literacy rate in the Bahamas is approximately 95.6 percent, which rivals that of developed countries and is considerably higher than the rate in most developing countries. Education is compulsory from ages five through sixteen.

The Bahamian education system is structured in a 6-3-3 format. Primary school lasts for six years for children aged five to ten. Secondary education is divided into two equal parts of three years each—junior high is for students aged eleven to fourteen, and senior high school is for students aged fourteen to seventeen. Although not yet mandatory, education at the preschool and post-secondary levels is rapidly expanding.

Four elementary school girls dressed in school uniforms whisper to each other in High Rock on Grand Bahama Island.

Students take periodic proficiency examinations at four stages. The Grade Level Assessment Tests (GLAT) are administered at the end of grades three and six. The Bahamas Junior Certificate is taken at the end of grade nine, and the Bahamas General Certificate of Secondary Education is an exit exam at the end of secondary school.

For tertiary, or post-secondary, education, there are two publically-funded universities and numerous private ones. In 2016, the College of the Bahamas (COB), founded in 1974, became the University of the Bahamas. Its main campuses are in New Providence, Grand Bahama, and San Salvador, with satellite campuses in Abaco and Exuma. Of its more than three hundred faculty members, about 75 percent are Bahamian. The Bahamas is also affiliated with the University of the West Indies (UWI), a public institution which has campuses in Barbados, Jamaica, and Trinidad. This university

Bahamians take advantage of the good medical care provided by public hospitals and clinics. But at the same time, many people—especially on the Family Islands—retain a strong belief in folk medicine to cure common ailments, and even some less common ones.

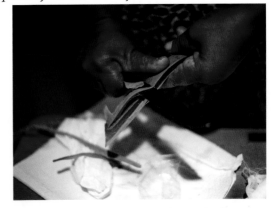

When used as a tea or in other liquid concoctions, for example, cerasee (Mormodica charantia) is said to be effective against anything from the common cold to cancer. The traditional Bahamian may believe that a poultice of pepper leaves reduces boils, dried goat droppings are effective against whooping cough, ground snails remove warts, and hog grease is a remedy for hair loss. Tea brewed from the leaves of a tree called the five-finger or chicken-toe tree is said to relieve body aches. Aloe vera, pictured above, soothes burns, and a salve of white sage leaves applied to the skin soothes chickenpox and measles. Wild guava is eaten by diabetics.

Of all the Family Islands, Cat Island is considered the stronghold of bush medicine, and many of the islanders there have the reputation of being effective healers. The island tradition in herbal remedies is included in the education program at the Rand Memorial Nature Center in Freeport, which displays exhibits and offers lectures on the subject.

serves some thirty-six thousand students in eighteen English-speaking countries or British Overseas Territories in the Caribbean.

HEALTH AND WELFARE

The government-run Bahamian health-care system covers the more populated islands. Nassau on New Providence has the largest public hospitals with state-of-the-art diagnostic equipment. Freeport on Grand Bahama has the government-run Rand Memorial Hospital. The other islands have clinics with resident doctors and nurses. Those who need specialist services not available in the Bahamas go to clinics in the United States, especially Florida,

POVERTY IN PARADISE

On islands often described as "paradise," the existence of poverty seems terribly out of place. Indeed, in most resorts, tourists are shielded from the harsh realities of poor Bahamians living not far away. After all, who would want to spend extravagantly in the casinos and expensive shops when faced with such need?

The Bahamas is often touted as one of the wealthiest of the Caribbean countries. It's true enough that the sort of abject deprivation common in some other Caribbean nations—particularly Haiti, but also Jamaica and others—is not usually seen here.

While statistics differ according to source, the CIA World Factbook states that 9.3 percent of the Bahamian population was living below the poverty line in 2010. By 2017, according to the Borgen Project, an international nonprofit group that fights extreme poverty, that figure had risen to 14.8 percent.

The Bahamas' lack of economic diversity makes it enormously dependent on tourism as its top employer. Some 49 percent of its people work directly or indirectly in that industry. The problem is that the majority of those jobs—particularly for young people—are unskilled labor paying minimum wage. Such jobs don't provide workers with the opportunity to advance or save money toward a better future.

Poverty has also ticked up as immigration has boomed. In fact, the majority of impoverished people in the Bahamas are from Haiti. It's unclear how many Haitians are living in the country, but estimates report they make up between 7.5 and 18 percent of the Bahamian population.

Perhaps surprisingly, climate change is another factor contributing to the Bahamas' poverty rate. As weather patterns become more extreme in the Bahamas, storms continue to create a considerable economic strain on the country. In 2017, for example, the unusually active hurricane season brought back-to-back hurricanes to the islands. Hurricanes Irma and Maria, both category 5 storms, slammed the Bahamas in September of that year. In fact, Irma was so powerful it sucked water away from beaches in the Bahamas, a rare weather phenomenon. Just one year earlier, Hurricane Matthew hit New Providence, the Bahamas' most populous island, head-on. It was the first major hurricane to strike Nassau since 1929. Damage from these recent storms has affected the nation's economy. Combined with poor infrastructure, the growing intensity of flooding and tropical storms has forced the government to raise spending on disaster relief.

usually through a referral by their doctors. Many doctors who practice in the Bahamas trained in medical colleges in the United States, Canada, or Britain, or at the University of the West Indies.

A mandatory government-run insurance plan provides retirement, disability, medical, maternity, and funeral insurance. Premiums are deducted from workers' salaries, and employers also make contributions. The ratio of payments by worker and employer varies with the salary.

THE IMPORTANCE OF MIAMI

The northern islands of the Bahamas lie close to the coast of Florida; the nearest islands, the Biminis, are only 50 miles (80 km) away. Since the early twentieth century, Americans have made the Biminis a vacation getaway, usually reaching the islands by yacht. The most famous of those was probably the American writer Ernest Hemingway, who described his experience in the Biminis in his novel *Islands in the Stream*. It was published in 1970, after Hemingway's death.

This aerial view of Bimini Island shows a high degree of development.

In recent years, the traffic has been in both directions. Making frequent trips across the narrow strip of the Atlantic dividing the two countries is the goal of many Bahamians. They may travel for a short holiday, for medical treatment at a hospital or clinic, or to visit friends, but the usual reason is to shop from the much wider selection of goods available on the American mainland. Clothes, electronic equipment, and housing materials are particularly in demand, and Bahamians can often be seen at the airport in Miami loaded down with such purchases. Import taxes in the Bahamas are extremely high and duty-free allowances comparatively low, so shopping is not a pastime that most Bahamians can indulge in nearly as often as they would like, but it explains why there are airplanes leaving every hour from Nassau to Miami.

Perhaps because many Bahamians have settled in southern Florida, one sees the Bahamian influence in the architecture of some houses there. Bahamian Village in Key West, an island off the Florida coast, has an annual celebration of Bahamian goombay music, while in Miami, a musical group called the Bahamas Junkanoo Revue creates Junkanoo costumes for its own parades and even participates in the Junkanoo parades in Nassau.

DO'S AND DON'TS

Bahamians are an extremely hospitable and friendly people. Whether on a Family Island or in Nassau, much of Bahamian life is lived outdoors, as the climate is quite dry and warm most of the year. It is common to see household members doing chores, visiting with friends, or just resting on the front porch. It is sociable to be outdoors, ready to greet neighbors and passersby, and to generally keep in touch with district affairs.

Showing respect to a casual acquaintance is important. The correct greeting is always appreciated. For example, identifying oneself clearly is important to a Bahamian; a stranger who fails to do so will most likely be asked where he or she comes from. Ignoring someone who is making friendly overtures is considered the height of bad form. Returning hospitality is important, from a verbal or written expression of gratitude to taking someone out for a meal.

Personal questions are the norm. Bahamians like to know all about people they meet. Yet they are seldom intrusive, for they also sense others' need for privacy. Their friendliness sometimes encourages people to make the mistake of being too open about other people and gossiping. Bahamians do this all the time with each other in fun, but jokes and gossip are shared only within their own circle.

However, despite their friendliness, eye contact is quite rare. Bahamians also strongly discourage staring, as they are at heart quite reserved and do not like being looked at aggressively.

INTERNET LINKS

https://www.ministryofeducationbahamas.com
The Ministry of Education site provides up-to-date information about schooling in the Bahamas.

https://www.ohchr.org/EN/NewsEvents/Pages/DisplayNews.aspx?NewsID=22554&LangID=E
The UN Human Rights Commission addresses violence against women in the Bahamas.

https://www.trubahamianfoodtours.com/tru-bahamian-must-eats/bush-teas
This site lists many bush tea remedies popular in the Bahamas.

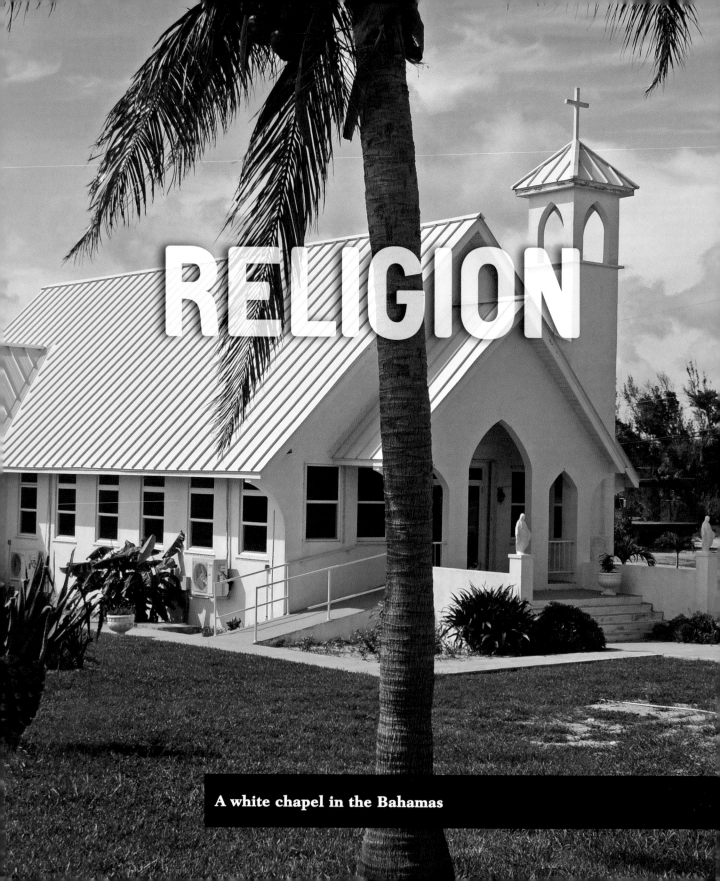

RELIGION

A white chapel in the Bahamas

CHRISTIANITY IS DOMINANT IN THE Bahamas. About 95 percent of the population practices some form of Protestantism, Catholicism, or another Christian religion. Indeed, the die was cast in 1492 when Christopher Columbus and his crew celebrated the "New World's" first Catholic Mass on San Salvador. The Protestant Eleutherans and British Loyalists who followed had converted their African slaves to Christianity, and the religion has held fast for generations of their descendents.

There are a few Muslims and even fewer Hindus, migrants who came to the Bahamas for work-related reasons, but they are dwarfed by both the size and the fervor of the Christian community.

THE IMPORTANCE OF CHRISTIANITY

Christianity in its various forms is a very important part of the fabric of daily life in the Bahamas. For almost all Bahamians, going to church on Sunday is the rule, and many people keep a Bible handy in a drawer at home or at work to read in their spare moments. Religious celebrations, both national and personal, often include big processions and displays.

THE FAITHS OF THE BAHAMAS

Many denominations of the Christian faith can be found on the islands. Christian Bahamians may be Anglicans, Baptists, Church of God, Mormons, Nazarenes, Jehovah's Witnesses, Methodists, Seventh-Day Adventists, Lutherans, or Roman Catholics. Churches run the gamut from almost cathedral-sized to small single-room buildings. No community worth its name would be without at least one church even if, as on the smaller islands, the minister has to go island-hopping by mail boat to hold services.

Many Bahamians like to participate unrestrainedly in the services of their chosen church. For instance, many Bahamian churches offer "testimony services" that give worshippers a chance to repent publicly of past sins and to seek forgiveness from the congregation as a whole.

OBEAH, MAGIC, AND SUPERSTITIONS

There is no apparent conflict between Bahamians' strict adherence to the Christian faith and their strong belief in supernatural spirits' ability to affect human lives. Such folk beliefs have been handed down through the generations and go back to the African ancestry of many black Bahamians. They are still practiced to some degree by even the most educated.

If a Bahamian thinks he has become the victim of some malicious spirit, he may mark a series of X's around himself and repeat the phrase "ten, ten, the Bible, ten" to offset the bad influence. Someone who is seriously concerned about an evil influence may also sprinkle a particular kind of seed called guinea grain around the place to keep malicious spirits so occupied (they have to pick up the seeds one by one, counting them as they do so) that they will not have time to do their evil work. Love potions are popular. "Cuckoo soup" is a dark-colored broth believed to have tremendous powers; one sip and the victim is hooked, no matter what his or her feelings were toward the perpetrator.

Many of these practices and beliefs fall under the imprecise heading of Obeah. This system of spiritual and healing practices, a blend of traditional West African rituals and Christian beliefs, developed in the eighteenth century among enslaved Africans throughout the Caribbean. Like other Afro-Caribbean religions, such as Vodou and Santería, it includes communication with ancestors and spirits and healing rituals involving talismans or charms. However, Obeah does not worship any particular canon of deities and has no institutionalized hierarchy.

Although Obeah is officially banned in the Bahamas, it is still possible to find some people who practice it. Obeah practitioners are well known in the community and even advertise under titles such as "spiritual healer" and "psychic adviser." They believe in their ability to control the lives of other people under certain circumstances. Naturally shed parts of a person (hair, fingernails) or even dirty laundry are thought to be sufficient material for an Obeah practitioner to put a spell or curse on a victim. The only remedy is to find someone with stronger powers to remove it.

There is both black (bad) and white (good) Obeah magic. An example of white magic is a dream book. Traditionalists keep one in the belief that good spirits will help them find prosperity, perhaps through winning a lottery by transmitting the winning numbers to them in their dreams. The dream book is to write down what numbers come to them when they sleep.

INTERNET LINKS

https://www.frommers.com/destinations/bahamas/in-depth/religion-myth--folklore
This travel site provides a quick overview of Obeah.

http://www.jabezcorner.com/grand_bahama/ten_ten1.html
The classic 1976 study, *Ten, Ten The Bible Ten: Obeah in the Bahamas*, is reprinted here.

http://www.tribune242.com/news/2017/apr/13/editorial-have-bahamians-returned-ten-ten-bible-te
This 2017 editorial discusses the interaction of modern-day Bahamian superstition and politics.

LANGUAGE

Women laugh together outside a church.

9

HAVING BEEN SETTLED PRIMARILY BY British and American migrants, it's natural that English is the official language of the Bahamas. That said, Bahamian English is distinctive in its own way. There are actually two English language forms used in the Bahamas—"standard" Bahamian English and a Bahamian dialect with a structure that draws heavily on those of various African languages.

The Bahamian dialect of English has the same musical rhythm found among other Caribbean islanders. Most Bahamians can speak both standard Bahamian English and the Bahamian dialect, crossing comfortably from one to the other. They usually know which one is more appropriate and apt for a particular situation.

There are also some French Creole speakers among the Haitian immigrants, but this language is very much confined to their own community, and very few Bahamians understand, much less speak, this special form of the language.

Bahamians can usually tell which island a fellow citizen is from just by the slight differences in the way he or she "talks Bahamian."

Here are some popular Bahamian slang terms and their meanings:

big-eye—*greedy*

biggety—*brash*

bright—*light skinned*

to buck up—*to crash a car*

Conchy Joe—*Bahamian of European descent*

cut hip—*to give a beating*

duff—*boiled, fruit-filled dough*

jack—*friend*

to jook—*to stab*

sip sip—*gossip*

sweetheart—*affair*

tree—*three*

TALKIN' BAHAMIAN

Standard Bahamian English follows the formal rules of British English—the Queen's English that is heard in Bahamian law courts, for example, or the English taught in schools. In those situations where standard English is appropriate, Bahamians speak with a distinctly British accent, as opposed to an American one, for example.

What makes the Bahamian spoken dialect in daily use unique is that it disregards many standard English rules. For example, the use of tenses often focuses on the present regardless of the period of time concerned: "I gone to work yesterday" sums up the past, while "We see you tomorrow" takes care of the future. Similarly, plurals are created simply by the context ("I have four nice dress"), and emphasis is provided through repetition ("That girl is pretty-pretty").

Bahamians also have some quite distinctive and unique words in their vocabulary, such as *boungy*, or buttocks, and *grabalishus*, which describes a greedy person. Some common English words show up in radically changed forms too. For instance it is quite possible in the Bahamas to catch "ammonia" (pneumonia) or even "browncurtis" (bronchitis).

Bahamian proverbs show a similar inventiveness of language. "It ain't for want of tongue that cow don't talk" means "Just because people have the ability to speak doesn't necessarily mean they always should." "The wind don't blow in the same dog tail all the time" means "Patience—your turn will come eventually."

All of this is spoken with a special lilt in the voice, often with a rising inflection at the end of a sentence and the addition of the word "eh" at the end if a question is being asked—"She be coming today, eh?"

A young man shares his knowledge of the sea.

PRONUNCIATION Standard English speakers may have to depend on context to follow a conversation in Bahamian patois (pa-twa), which is another word for dialect or informal regional speech. In fast-paced dialogue, words lose their consonants, have their vowels changed, or are otherwise rearranged by a transposition of letters. For example, "them" becomes *dem*, "woman" is *ooman*, "man" is *mon*, "film" is *flim*, "you" is *yo*, "thought" is *tot*, and "smash" is *mash*. In addition, endings are lost, so that "cleaning" becomes *cleanin'*, "don't" is *dun*, and "child" is *chile*. Those accustomed to Jamaican patois will have little trouble, since the Bahamian version is more recognizable to the standard English speaker than Jamaican.

It's worth noting that speaking dialect is not a sign of laziness or ignorance. Bahamian English has its own internal structure, rules, and sensibility. For example, the *h* sound is often dropped in spoken form, so that "thanks" becomes *t'anks*, and "house" becomes *'ouse*. On the other hand, some words replace the *th* sound with a *d* sound, so that "that" and "them" become *dat* and *dem*. The language incorporates African grammatical influences and in some cases, an older style of Puritan English. All this combines into a unique and lively language that richly reflects the heritage of the people and the place.

THE MAN WHO WROTE THE BAHAMIAN ENGLISH DICTIONARY

In 1982, John A. Holm published the first Dictionary of Bahamian English *with his colleague Alison W. Shilling. Holm, an American linguist, compiled the dictionary while working as a linguistics professor at the College of the Bahamas from 1978 to 1980. Although the book is now out of print, older volumes are still available for sale and the book can be accessed electronically online.*

Linguistics is the scientific study of languages, and Holm was a very influential scientist. He changed how linguists view languages such as Bahamian English. After compiling the first (and only) dictionary of the Bahamian dialect, he published a two-volume landmark study, Pidgins and Creoles *in 1988 and 1989. Linguists use those terms, along with others—including patois, dialect, jargon, and vernacular—to describe different kinds of nonstandard languages. In his study, Holm traced the evolution of more than one hundred such languages and their variations, and proved they were languages in their own right, reflecting a variety of historical and geographical influences.*

Prior to Holm's work, such "nonstandard" languages were considered merely bastardized, or corrupted, illegitimate versions of European languages, not worthy of academic study. The fact that these languages are largely spoken by poor people of color further degraded their status among many linguists.

Holm, who died in 2016, opened the field of linguists to vibrant new areas of study, and he fostered a broader sense of respect for all human cultures and the forces of history that inform them.

KEEPIN' UP WIT' DA NEWS

Considering the widespread geographical nature of the country, continuous access to the media plays a most important part in keeping Bahamians entertained and up to date about current events in the Bahamas and the rest of the world.

Radio Bahamas broadcasts throughout all the Bahamian islands nonstop via four stations, each offering different programming or focusing on a different geographic area. There are also two privately owned radio stations. On some islands, however, it is easier to tune in to Florida stations. There is also a television service by the Bahamas Broadcasting Corporation, which offers programming twenty-four hours a day, seven days a week. In addition, most Bahamians have access to a wide range of programs from the United States using satellite dishes or by subscribing to cable networks.

The Nassau Guardian and the Tribune are major newspapers published in Nassau and available on all the major islands. Two daily newspapers, the Bahama Journal and the Freeport News, are published in Freeport. But most Bahamians outside the major centers rely much more on electronic media than they do on newspapers, for the news is old by the time newspapers arrive by mail boat at some of the more remote islands.

INTERNET LINKS

https://www.nassauparadiseisland.com/talk-like-a-bahamian -island-terms-and-phrases
This site lists some commonly used Bahamian phrases and their meanings.

https://www.nytimes.com/2016/01/04/us/john-holm-pioneer-in -lingustics-dies-at-72.html
The obituary for John Holm provides insight into his influence on linguists.

ARTS

A goombay drummer pounds out a rhythm in a nightclub in Nassau.

10

THE ARTS OF THE BAHAMAS ARE AN exuberant mix of African, American, and European heritage. This blend characterizes Caribbean arts in general, and yet it somehow is uniquely Bahamian as well. Music and dance are especially important, and both grow out of the African storytelling tradition. Bahamian storytellers weave morals and myths into musical folktales. They call this musical improvisation ad-libbing, rigging, or chatting and use it not only for entertainment but also in church.

Goombay is said to be derived from the African word *nkumbi*. In the Bantu language, it describes a type of ceremonial drum. Goombay drums, used at the Junkanoo and goombay festivals, have been traced to West African djembe drums.

MUSIC AND DANCE

Bahamians love to sing and dance, and they do both with tremendous enthusiasm. The annual Junkanoo parades feature dancing and the most popular form of Bahamian music, goombay.

GOOMBAY On the islands the beat of goatskin drums accompanied by bongos, conch-shell horns, maracas, rattles, "click" sticks, flutes, bugles, whistles, and cowbells can be heard year-round in both

A costumed horn player takes part in Nassau's Junkanoo festivities on January 1, 2014.

impromptu and rehearsed performances. The different renditions of goombay are unique; the only common thread running through them all is a fast-paced, regular, and sustained melody.

Goombay music was imported a few centuries ago with the enslaved peoples from the west coast of Africa. It is a mixture of rhythmic African drumming ("talking drums" were used to communicate over distances) and traditional slave songs developed during the many years of black oppression in North America. This percussion music was made famous by Blake Alphonso "Blind Blake" Higgs (1915—1986), who played to tourists arriving at Nassau (now Lynden Pindling) International Airport for several years.

Today, goombay music is commercially packaged in all the tourist hotels, where colorful, ruffle-sleeved dancers (usually male) gyrating to the goombay beat are the expected entertainment. As it is a part of the Junkanoo festival in December, people sometimes refer to it, incorrectly, as Junkanoo music. Every summer, beginning around June, the islands reverberate in a four-month-long goombay festival. One popular goombay musician and painter was Tony McKay (1942—1997), also known as Exuma, the Obeah Man. Something of a cult figure, he was known for his outrageous costumes and long, braided hair.

RAKE 'N' SCRAPE Another kind of music found throughout the islands, usually played in bars and clubs and during festivals and regattas, is rake 'n' scrape. This is impromptu music played on accordions and guitars, usually accompanied by a variety of homemade instruments ranging from shakers made of seed-filled pods to saws played with household implements.

REGGAE, RAP, SOCA, CALYPSO, HIP-HOP, AND R&B These are among the other popular muscial styles that have emerged in the Bahamas in recent decades. They are often integrated with goombay sounds. Reggae and calypso are sounds associated with Jamaica, while soca is a Caribbean dance music with a pounding beat derived from calypso and American soul music.

SPIRITUALS Church music is close to the Bahamian soul. Attending church and participating in the choir are very important to Bahamians, so most churches have a well-developed choral music tradition. Spirituals brought to the Bahamas by enslaved people from North America are prominently featured. There are many variants of these, including the call-and-answer type of singing in which the choir and the congregation exchange questions and answers in song—this is the chatting or rigging that is part of Bahamian music.

The fire dance in the Bahamas has become a thing of the past, but before the 1940s, African Bahamians used to congregate at night by fires to sing and dance. Dances were often secret, as they were considered wild and un-Christian. However, fire dances eventually became a tourist attraction, and are still performed. The dancers carry and dance with fire, performing dangerous movements in a sensuous manner.

LITERATURE

Recently, a growing number of books have been written by Bahamians about the Bahamas. Among the most popular of these are several books by Patricia Glinton-Meicholas on Bahamian life and culture, especially *How to Be a True-True Bahamian* and *Talkin' Bahamian*. Although only partly about the Bahamas, the actor Sidney Poitier's autobiography, *This Life*, offers insights into life on Cat Island, where he was born and raised. Another Bahamian autobiography that islanders enjoy reading is Leonard Thompson's *I Wanted Wings*. Marion Bethel (b. 1953) is a well-known Bahamian poet whose writing has appeared in American literary journals. She was awarded the Casa de las Americas Prize in 1994 for her book of poems *Guanahani, My Love*. Today, she lives in Nassau. The prolific Obediah Michael Smith (b. 1954) has published twenty books of poetry, most recently *Women in Ninja* (2015) which refers to an eastern region in Uganda. Since 2014, Smith has been traveling around Africa.

Perhaps the most famous Bahamian of the twentieth century is the actor, director, diplomat, writer, and civil rights activist Sidney Poitier (b. 1927). By chance, Poitier was born in Florida, which automatically made him a US citizen, but he was really Bahamian. His parents were farmers who lived on Cat Island in the Bahamas. They regularly traveled to Miami to sell their produce, and while there in 1927, pregnant with her eighth child, Poitier's mother went into labor two months early. Young Sidney grew up on Cat Island, with no formal education, and without electricity, plumbing, or other modern conveniences, until he was ten years old.

On sparsely populated, nearly all-black Cat Island, Sidney never experienced racial differences. It wasn't until he moved to Miami at age fifteen that he encountered racism. The young man eventually ended up acting in theater productions, and then movies. At the time, Hollywood rarely used black actors for any roles other than servants, which Poitier refused to play.

His breakout role was in the controversial, landmark film Blackboard Jungle *(1955) in which he played a rebellious high school student. With his good looks, intelligence, superb acting, and eloquent diction—he trained the Caribbean accent out of his speech—and because of the great care he took about the roles he accepted, Poitier went on to become one of the most popular actors—and the leading African American actor—of the mid-century era. Some of his most successful films were* The Defiant Ones *(1958),* A Patch of Blue *(1965),* To Sir, with Love *(1967),* In the Heat of the Night *(1967), and* Guess Who's Coming to Dinner *(1967). He was the first African American man to win a competitive Oscar for his role in* Lilies of the Field *(1963). Many of these films were trailblazing movies that explored racial issues which had previously been avoided in American filmmaking. Although Poitier was sometimes criticized for playing the "idealized" or "perfect" black man—a restriction he found frustrating—it was what American culture (and predominantly white audiences) of the time seemed to require.*

Poitier has earned a long list of awards and honors. In 1974, he was knighted by Queen Elizabeth; therefore, he is entitled to be known as Sir Sidney Poitier, but does not himself use the title. In 1999, the American Film Institute named him as one of the twenty-five "Greatest Male Stars" of classic Hollywood cinema. In 2001, he was awarded a lifetime achievement Academy Award for "his remarkable accomplishments as an artist and as a human being."

Later in his life, Poitier served as ambassador to Japan for the Bahamas from 1997 to 2007. He also wrote two memoirs and other books. In 2009, President Barack Obama, above, awarded him the US Presidential Medal of Freedom.

VISUAL ARTS

Painting is a flourishing art form in the Bahamas. Many contemporary Bahamian artists use their surroundings as their inspiration, painting landscapes and seascapes, Bahamian houses, Junkanoo dancers and musicians, and other Bahamians in brightly colored settings.

A leading folk artist who inspired young Bahamian artists was Amos Ferguson (1920—2009), whose primitive oils on cardboard carry four main themes: history, religion, nature, and folklore. Antonius Roberts (b. 1958) is a noted Bahamian artist and sculptor who is also an environmentalist. Eric Ellis (b. 1964) is a painter (and policeman!) from Exuma whose work is closely related to Junkanoo and Bahamian culture.

Brent Malone (1941—2004), often called the "father of Bahamian art," began as a potter and went on to become a renowned painter and gallery owner dedicated to promoting Bahamian art. His efforts helped to free Bahamian artists from feeling restricted by the need to produce "postcard" images of pretty scenery to sell to the tourist market.

Other noteworthy artists from the Bahamas include Jackson Burnside, Dave Smith, Eddie Minnis, John Beadle, John Cox, Kendal Hanna, Max Taylor, and Stan Burnside.

HANDICRAFTS

Traditional handicrafts have always been a part of the Bahamian lifestyle. With increasing tourist arrivals, crafts have become an important local industry. Particularly at the Nassau Straw Market, visitors can find a wide

Handcrafts of all sorts are displayed at the famous **Nassau Straw Market.**

range of products shipped there from other Bahamian islands. The most popular items are manufactured from natural materials such as straw dried from wild grasses. Straw products include bags, hats, baskets, dolls, place mats, floor mats, and other household items. Most of these are handmade, a simple sewing machine being the only mechanical equipment used.

Hardwood carvings and small pieces of furniture are popular as well. Local artists also make ceramic pottery. Tourists buy tumblers and figurines, some signed by famous artists such as Amos Ferguson, as souvenirs.

INTERNET LINKS

http://www.amosfergusonartgallery.com
Information about and paintings by Amos Ferguson can be found on this site.

https://www.daguilarartfoundation.com
This Nassau-based foundation focuses on Bahamian visual arts.

https://folkways.si.edu (search Genre: Caribbean; Country, Bahamas)
The Smithsonian Folkways Recordings collection includes 162 albums of historical Bahamian music which can be sampled online.

http://nagb.org.bs
This is the site of the National Art Gallery of the Bahamas.

https://www.vanityfair.com/hollywood/2017/02/sidney-poitier -remarkable-run-in-hollywood-history
This article looks at the extraordinary achievements of Sidney Poitier.

LEISURE

A stolid flycatcher sits on a branch on Paradise Island.
The Bahamas is an excellent country for bird-watching.

11

I N A COUNTRY THAT SEEMS TO EXIST primarily for recreation, fun, and relaxation, there's no shortage of things to do. Tourists flock to these islands for just that purpose, but the Bahamian people likewise enjoy the advantages their homeland has to offer. The nearly perfect Bahamian climate encourages people to spend much of their leisure time outdoors. With such easy access to the sea and lovely beaches close at hand, many leisure activities are water-related, although there are lots of attractions on land as well.

For the average working person or school kid in the Bahamas, however, leisure time is mainly spent much like it is anywhere—just chilling with friends, visiting with family, watching TV, listening to music, reading, catching a game, or just doing whatever feels right and restful.

SWIMMING AND BEACHES

Most beaches in the Bahamas are pristine, with white sand so fine it feels soft to the touch. Harbour Island, though, is renowned for its pink-sand beaches—the pink color comes from shells and coral crushed by the waves over the years.

The Bahamas is one of the world's best places to go bird-watching. There are numerous nature reserves that are protected habitats for more than five thousand bird species, one of the most spectacular being the Bahamian national bird, the pink flamingo.

Beaches throughout the Bahamas often feature shallow, transparent water for hundreds of yards out to sea, rising gently to sandbars before finally dropping into the depths. The hotel beaches are beautifully maintained, and many of them offer access to inshore coral reefs, enabling the more timid to enjoy the experience of snorkeling without having to venture too far into the water.

BOATING AND SAILING

Bahamian residents enjoy spending their time on top of the water as well as in it, so boating in vessels of all shapes and sizes is quite popular. A good number of Bahamians own boats and use them for a variety of purposes, often chartering them out to the tourists for island touring or deep-sea sport fishing.

Regattas (sailboat races) take place year-round and attract competitive sailors from all over the world. The races are a great excuse for a party, and

A sailor gets his boat ready for the next race in the Little Farmer's Cay Regatta.

while the main show is the regatta itself, accompanying events back on shore may include live entertainment, art shows, beauty pageants, and cooking demonstrations. Other events include pineapple festivals, conch-cracking contests, and historical weekends to celebrate Loyalist roots. In all of these, music and food are always prominently featured.

The National Family Island Regatta, for example, is held each year during the last full week of April. Now one of the oldest regattas in the Bahamas, the event began in 1954 with the main goal of preserving the boatbuilding skills of Bahamian sailors. The tradition has continued, and today sailors from every major island in the country compete for the honor and the glory. Classes A to E boats compete in cup and series races to win the big trophy.

According to the rules, the boats must be designed, built, owned, and sailed by Bahamians. They try to use materials that preserve the traditions of the early boat-builders as much as possible. Sailing fans from all over gather in George Town on Exuma Island for the five-day event, taking in the beauty of white sails against the blue sea and sky.

DIVING AND SNORKELING

The islands are a diving and snorkeling paradise. Many local companies cater to people who want to learn or practice either activity. It is easy to see the attraction of scuba diving for both locals and tourists, as the sea around the islands is full of exotic marine life and numerous old wrecks whose nooks and crannies make interesting places to explore. The water temperature remains constant year-round, which means it is possible to dive without a wet suit at any time. The underwater visibility is usually exceptionally good.

Experienced scuba-diving enthusiasts like to try wall or cave diving, although neither is for the more cautious, as they often involve descents of more than 100 feet (30 m) in order to get into one of the underwater caves or blue holes. Snorkeling is a less dangerous pastime and requires only a mask, a breathing tube, and flippers. Swimming near the surface of one of the many Bahamian coral reefs, the snorkeler can see a colorful variety of marine life, ranging from moray eels and turtles to angelfish and parrot fish. For those who want to join in and swim with some of the bigger fish but are

not prepared to scuba dive or snorkel on their own, a number of Bahamian companies offer experiences such as swimming with dolphins or even sharks.

For those who would like to see the seabed but find scuba diving too adventurous, there is helmet diving. The helmet diver takes a walk along the seabed with a helmet on top of his head, into which is pumped a constant supply of fresh air from the diving boat. The diver's head stays dry, and he can wear contact lenses or adjust his glasses underwater. Each helmet dive lasts approximately a half-hour.

FISHING

Fishing is popular with both Bahamians and tourists. There are many possibilities, ranging from using a simple hook and line to working with all the complex gear of a deep-sea fishing expedition.

CASINOS AND GAMBLING

Gambling occupies a very curious legal and social position in the Bahamas. In short, foreign tourists may gamble, but Bahamian residents may not—at least, not legally.

Gambling is one of those adult activities that many people enjoy but that can lead to trouble. People play various betting games in hope of winning great riches. This rarely happens, however; it's much more typical that gamblers lose their money. For many folks, it's harmless fun; but for others, gambling can easily become an addiction, leading to financial ruin and personal devastation. Gambling also attracts gangsters, crime, and corruption.

A great deal of money changes hands at casinos and other gambling venues, and for that reason, governments regulate and tax such activities. In the Bahamas, gambling was illegal through most of the twentieth century. However, in the 1960s, after the Cuban Revolution shut down the infamous casinos of Havana, attention shifted to the Bahamas, right next door. As tourism grew and resorts sprang up, the gambling ban presented a problem. Top international hoteliers wanted to include casinos in their luxurious resorts— after all, there were enormous profits to be made!

The Bahamian government was eager for the influx of tax monies, but the powerful Bahamian churches were strongly opposed to the influx of vice. In the end, a compromise resulted in the current state of affairs. Fancy casinos pull out all the stops to attract foreigners and encourage them to lay their money down. Meanwhile, Bahamians—many of whom work in those casinos—are barred from gambling.

But that's not the end of the story. It's well known that another form of gambling exists outside the tourist zones. Illegal numbers rackets and web shops are patronized by many Bahamians, with only the occasional legal crackdown.

In a 2013 national referendum—with, it has been noted, a low voter turnout— Bahamians rejected proposals to legalize gambling by islanders. The Bahamas therefore continues to stand almost alone in the world, with the exception of several Islamic countries, in allowing gambling for tourists but not for residents.

A fisherman casts his line for bonefish on the reef in the Andros Islands.

The bonefish is highly sought after in the Bahamas, which has the largest concentration of bonefish in the world. These large-eyed, very bony fish can weigh from 5 to 10 pounds (2.3 to 4.5 kg) and be more than a foot (30 cm) long. They are challenging to catch, as they never stay in one place long and are extremely sensitive to sound.

Bigger fish that provide sport for Bahamian fishermen include wahoo (many local tournaments are dedicated to catching wahoo), snapper, grouper, and marlin. Sport fishing is quite tightly regulated in Bahamian waters. Permits are needed for deep-sea fishing, and there are limits on how much fish can be caught by a single angler. There is no lack of charter boats to take enthusiasts to deeper waters to fish for sport fish such as the large blue marlin and tuna.

LAND SPORTS

The number of golf courses has increased dramatically during the past few years. It is now possible to play golf on most of the inhabited islands of the Bahamas, although New Providence and Grand Bahama have the most prominent courses. Clubs organize tournaments regularly, and the Bahamas hosts leading international tournaments.

With the country's British heritage, cricket was once quite popular, but Bahamian enthusiasm for the sport has fallen off since independence. Since the 1970s, it has given way to more American-oriented sports such as baseball, basketball, softball, and football.

HIKING, CYCLING, AND RIDING

The islands have coastal trails, and there are tracks running through many nature reserves, but the inland terrain is generally rough and overgrown with bushes. Hikers have to beware of sinkholes concealed beneath low bushes. Cycling and riding are less common on the islands, except at a few resorts that provide good roads for cyclists. However, Grand Bahama hosts a 100-mile (161-km) road race for cycling enthusiasts every year, while an organization on Eleuthera organizes weeklong cycling trips. Mountain bikes fare better on the rough Bahamian terrain.

TRADITIONAL PASTIMES

Traditional games such as *warri* (WAR-ee) are part of the African heritage of the majority of Bahamians. Dominoes, checkers, and many varieties of card games are also still popular. Storytelling is an important part of the Bahamian leisure tradition. The telling of tales of magic and supernatural heroes has died out, but tales based on family history and local events, especially tales of disaster, are commonplace and appreciated by both young and old.

A group of Bahamian men play dominoes at an airport on Acklins Island as they wait for a plane from Nassau to arrive.

INTERNET LINKS

https://www.bahamas.com/things-do
This travel site lists many activities for tourists.

http://www.bahamas.gov.bs/mysc
This is the government portal page of the Ministry of Youth, Sports, and Culture.

FESTIVALS

The leader of a Junkanoo dance troupe smiles in her brightly colored costume.

12

HOLIDAYS ARE OCCASIONS FOR extended Bahamian families to gather for a special homecoming celebration, with feasts, parties, songs, and long sessions of storytelling. In true Caribbean style, Bahamian festivals are lavish, long-lasting, and loud. Most of them tie in with Christian festivals, and some are expressions of national pride. But none exemplify the Bahamian spirit better than the Christmas and New Year's festival no true-true Bahamian would miss— Junkanoo.

Bahamians spend months preparing their costumes for Junkanoo. The results are so spectacular that some of the best ones are displayed in the Junkanoo Expo Museum and the Educulture Bahamas Junkanoo Museum, both in Nassau.

JUNKANOO

Junkanoo is a festival celebrated throughout the Caribbean—in Jamaica, it's called Jonkonnu—which takes place around Christmas and New Year's. The tradition is associated with Christmas because, in the seventeenth century, that was the only time of the year that the slaves were allowed to have a holiday.

Participants in this vibrant street parade dress up in a dazzling variety of colorful costumes, known as scrap, complete with hats and masks representing mythical and imaginary characters. They parade down the length of Bay Street in Nassau—the biggest Junkanoo parade in the Bahamas—and the main streets of smaller towns. The marchers dance to the accompaniment of goombay music made with goatskin drums, gourds, cowbells, conches, horns, and whistles. The crowds lining the streets join in with or without instruments, imitating the *ka-lik ka-lik* sound of the cowbells. The object is to be as flamboyant and to make as much noise as possible.

No one knows for certain how this festival got its name, although some have suggested that it was named after John (Johnny) Canoe, an African folk hero and tribal chief who lived in the early 1700s. His true name is unknown but he is sometimes referred to as John Kenu or January (Jan) Conny. He demanded the right to celebrate with his people even after being made a slave.

Another theory is that the name came from the French phrase *gens inconnus* (zhohn en-kon-OO), meaning alien or unknown people. If this is true, it is appropriate for this festival because participants in a Junkanoo

This parade reveler's intricately decorated costume depicts an elephant.

parade are masked to conceal their identity, similar to what happens during the celebration of Mardi Gras in the United States.

Preparations for Junkanoo begin up to a year before the first "rush," as each parade is known, and are often very elaborate. Most of the participants belong to one of the many competing groups sanctioned by the national Junkanoo committee, which awards prizes for the best costumes and music. These groups—which can sometimes number up to five hundred members and which give themselves names such as Saxons, Pigs, Valley Boys, and Music Makers—usually decide well in advance on a theme that will be reflected in the costumes of their members. The exact details of what everyone will be wearing and what they will represent are closely guarded secrets until they assemble for the parade.

Individuals can also take part in the Junkanoo procession, and their costumes are every bit as fanciful as the group ones though usually not as elaborate. There are minimum requirements for costumes in a Junkanoo parade, but usually the more colorful and fantastic the better.

Cardboard and crepe paper are common construction materials for the Junkanoo costumes, and paint and "tricks"—beads, satin, and plastic jewels among them—are used to embellish them. Because of the fragile nature of such materials, however, and the exuberance with which their wearers move about during the parade itself, many costumes do not survive the parade in very good condition. Fortunately, the best of them have been preserved by collectors, and many are on display in the National Junkanoo Museum, a recent feature of the Nassau waterfront.

The first parade begins at 3 or 4 a.m. on Boxing Day, the day after Christmas, with streetlights shining on a sea of strange and wonderful characters. During the parade, participants stop and perform their dances at designated places along the route, while the drummers show off their amazing skill. This is called a breakout. When the parade continues, spectators join in, dancing to the music behind the performers. When the dancing ends, people gather for the prize-giving, after which the celebration draws to a close at about dawn. People straggle home exhausted, to recoup their energy for the second rush, on New Year's Day.

THE GOOMBAY SUMMER FESTIVAL

There are many reflections of the Junkanoo experience at other times of the year besides December and January. One of the hotels even sponsors a mini Junkanoo procession every Friday night. Nothing comes close to the actual winter celebration, but one of the best replicas is the Goombay Summer Festival, which combines the exuberance of a Junkanoo procession with goombay music performances. The traditional festival highlights the islands' local foods, crafts, and entertainment, and is aimed at increasing tourism and economic growth.

NATIONAL HOLIDAYS

Among the public holidays are Bahamian Independence Day and Emancipation Day. Independence Day is on July 10, but the celebration lasts a week, with speeches, parades, and fireworks. Emancipation Day, observed on the first Monday in August, celebrates the anniversary of the freeing of slaves throughout the British colonies. In Nassau, the end of slavery is also celebrated during Fox Hill Day, which takes place on the second Tuesday in August. Fox Hill Day owes its origin to the fact that it took about ten days for news of freedom from slavery to reach the then somewhat isolated community of Fox Hill.

Another national holiday was once called Discovery Day, October 12, which commemorated the landing of Christopher Columbus on the island of San Salvador in 1492. Discovery Day was renamed National Heroes' Day in 2002, to honor outstanding people who made contributions that altered the course of Bahamian history or gave service to the Bahamas. Among the people honored during the first National Heroes' Day were Sir Lynden Oscar Pindling, the "father of the nation," who was the chief architect of the modern-day Bahamas, and Dame Doris Johnson, the first woman to run for parliament, the first female senator, the first female minister in government, and the first female leader of the Senate.

Other national holidays include Majority Rule Day, January 10, which became a public holiday in 2014. It commemorates the day in 1967 when the

Bahamas gained majority rule for the first time—a step toward its eventual independence from Great Britain in 1973.

Randal Fawkes Labour Day is a version of other countries' Labor Day, a public holiday honoring workers and labor unions. In the Bahamas, it is held the first Friday of June and is named in memory of Sir Randal Fawkes (1924—2000), a Bahamian politician, trade unionist, and lawyer.

CHRISTMAS AND EASTER

Christmas in the Bahamas is celebrated much as it is elsewhere, without snow, of course. Christmas markets open in advance of the holiday for gift shopping, and the day itself is a family and church affair. A typical Bahamian Christmas meal consists of baked ham and roasted turkey with stuffing, peas 'n' rice, yam or sweet potato, baked macaroni and cheese, potato salad, coleslaw, and vegetables. Conch dishes are typical, as well as garlic pork and pepper pot. Dessert is often black cake, a dark spicy fruit and nut cake doused in rum that is popular throughout the Caribbean islands at Christmastime.

Easter is celebrated in Nassau with parties and Easter egg hunts. The holiday weekend includes Good Friday and Easter Monday. Whit Monday is celebrated seven weeks after Easter, a movable feast day that depends on the date of Easter.

INTERNET LINKS

http://creativenassau.com/junkanoo
This arts and culture site offers a timeline and bright photos relating to Junkanoo.

https://www.timeanddate.com/holidays/bahamas
This calendar site lists the holidays and observances in the Bahamas.

http://www.tourismtoday.com/events
The Ministry of Tourism site offers listings of events relating to a wide range of Bahamian festivals, holidays, and celebrations.

FOOD

Tomatoes, limes, and chilies on display at a market are the makings of a conch salad.

13

BEING ISLANDERS, THE ORIGINAL Bahamian people, the Lucayans, relied largely on seafood. This they supplemented with cassava, corn, and sweet potatoes, all of which are native to the Bahamas. The Lucayans are long gone, but the waves of new inhabitants have left their mark on the island diet. Today, British meat pies and roasts are still popular, and North American cuisine, especially the foods of the American South, play an important part in Bahamian cuisine. The African influence, which is reflected in many of those dishes, is present in grits, johnnycakes, and peas 'n' rice, as well as in the flavorings. Bahamian seasonings include salt, nutmeg, ginger, chili peppers, lime, parsley, thyme, and tarragon.

Turtle soup was once popular in the Bahamas, but new environmental protection laws have banned it. The Bahamas' shallow seagrass beds and reefs are prime foraging grounds for big, slow sea turtles, but overfishing—along with pollution and development—has endangered the populations. Old-timers on some of the outer islands still make the soup, and some tourists seek it out, but it's a dying tradition.

Coral-colored conch shells are treasured for their spiraled beauty, as well as for the animals that live within.

CONCH

Although seafood in general plays a big part in the modern islanders' diet, none is more iconically Bahamian than the conch. Conch is a snail-like mollusk found all over the Bahamas, and its white, pink-fringed meat forms the basis of many dishes. It can be fried, grilled, steamed, stewed, or made into a raw conch salad, the conch meat diced and mixed with chopped onion, tomato, cucumber, and celery, then liberally sprinkled with pepper and lime juice.

After a first taste, a newcomer might wonder why a not particularly appetizing meat is eaten by Bahamians in so many ways—from gourmet dishes in fancy restaurants to conch fritters called cracked conch sold at small stalls on sidewalks. Mainly, it's popular because it is indigenous to the islands, inexpensive, rich in protein, and versatile.

However, the once plentiful sea animals are disappearing from Bahamian ocean waters. The population of queen conch has suffered a major decline over the past twenty years or so, with researchers reporting a severe shortage of juvenile conchs in the local marine environment. Overfishing is thought to be a major cause—the animal is prized not only as food, but also for the beauty of its shells. Its importance to the Bahamian economy and culture is enormous. The coral-pink queen conch shell crowns the nation's coat of arms.

A conch cracking contest is held on National Heroes' Day. Conch cracking requires dexterity in removing the meat: the cracker first hits the shell with a heavy implement to break it (it must be hit in the right spot, where the meat is attached to the shell), then "jewks" the conch out of its shell by grasping an appendage (commonly called a foot or a claw) and pulling it.

OTHER SEAFOOD

Rock lobster, also called spiny lobster or crawfish, is also very popular, as is the land crab, which can be seen running around on many of the islands and is easily caught. It is often served stuffed with other food. From among the large variety of fish caught off the Bahamian coasts, grouper, a mild-flavored whitefish, is a particular favorite. This is often served with a spicy Creole-style sauce, followed closely by baked bonefish with a hot pepper sauce. Outside the more populated centers, many other varieties of seafood find their way to the table—turtle dishes are popular on the Exumas, for instance, while in other areas recipes can feature such marine life as yellowtail, snapper, grunt, jack, and even goggle-eye.

One of the most common ways of preparing fish, especially for breakfast, is "boil fish" or "stew fish," a kind of stew in which a firm-fleshed fish (often grouper) is put in the pot with salt pork, onions, potatoes, celery, tomatoes, and seasonings and then boiled until the appetizing aroma is sufficiently strong to tempt the cook to tuck into sizable helpings of the end result.

A live conch hangs out of its shell.

GRITS, PEAS, AND JOHNNYCAKE

Seafood and other meats are often eaten with side dishes, including some of the most traditional of all Afro-Bahamian foods: grits, peas 'n' rice, and johnnycake. All three are quite similar in appearance to dishes eaten in the southern United States, and indeed many of these recipes came over from the American South with the enslaved ancestors of today's Bahamians.

A generous mound of grits, ground cornmeal mush, with vegetables added often forms the basis of a meal. There are as many recipes for peas 'n' rice as there are people, for they depend on the individual blending of ingredients, the cooking time, and the sauces poured over them. Ingredients can range from simply pigeon peas (not green peas) and rice to pigeon peas and rice with salt pork, tomatoes, thyme, green pepper, celery, or virtually any other

Fish and grits, Bahama style, is a favorite dish.

ingredients an inspired cook might choose to add. As for seasonings, individual taste dictates what these should be, common ones being salt, whole peppercorns, allspice, chili peppers, and chopped onions.

Johnnycake, once considered a poor man's food because it was the staple diet of impoverished early settlers, is a pan-baked bread made with milk, butter, flour, sugar, salt, and baking powder. Sometimes it is even baked in a sand-filled box on fishing boats. Johnnycake tastes rather bland, but it certainly fills the stomach.

SOUSE

A popular dish in the Bahamas, especially on the weekend, is souse. It is popular because of its ability to fill an empty stomach while requiring very little work from the cook. The meat ingredients can be anything: parts of a sheep, including the tongue; parts of a pig, including the trotters; chicken; or conch. These are tossed into a large pot of salted water and boiled with spices and other ingredients. When the meat is tender enough to eat, it is ladled onto plates, liberally sprinkled with lime juice and pepper, and eaten with bread.

This steaming dish of souse is made with pigs' feet.

There are different kinds of souse. In England, the meat parts (trotters and ears, for instance) are pickled in vinegar. In the Bahamas, however, spices are used in the cooking, and lime juice is added when serving to give it a sour flavor.

DESSERTS

Dessert often incorporates tropical fruits or coconut. By far the absolute favorite dish is guava duff. A duff is a boiled pudding (not an American-style creamy pudding, but the cakelike British style) filled with fruit—usually guava, but it could be melon, pineapple, papaya, or mango—and eaten with a sweet sauce. Good Bahamian cooks have their own recipe, often handed

A ripe soursop
is ready to
be enjoyed. down for generations and jealously guarded. A good guava duff is time-consuming to make.

TROPICAL FRUIT

Many varieties of locally grown fruit are eaten raw or form the basis of desserts and drinks. Some of these, such as bananas, papayas, pineapples, and mangoes, are also popular outside the Bahamas. Others, including soursops, sugar apples (also called sweetsops or custard apples), sapodillas, and jujubes, have flavors that may be unknown to people in more northern climates.

The dark green, irregularly shaped soursop is covered with soft spines and weighs from 1 to 5 pounds (0.5 to 2.3 kg). Its fibrous white pulp is refreshing;

far from being sour, it is usually sweet with only a slightly tart flavor. The sugar apple belongs to the same family as the soursop. It looks like a green (sometimes purplish brown) pinecone about the size of a tennis ball. To eat it, one splits the soft fruit open by hand and spoons out its sweet, smooth, segmented white flesh, separating it from the shiny black seeds.

The sapodilla is an oval, brown fruit about 2 to 3 inches (5 to 8 cm) across, with three to six black seeds. The flesh, which is pale brown and smooth but sometimes slightly grainy, has been likened to that of pear flavored with brown sugar.

DRINKS

Drinks in the Bahamas tend to fall into two categories—those concocted for and served mainly to the tourists who frequent casino resorts and those consumed by the locals. Those in the first category are often based on varieties of rum.

For nonalcoholic drinks, Bahamians prefer those that are typically refreshing in hot climates—fresh lime coolers, for instance, and the more traditional sodas such as cola and ginger ale. Fruit juices are quite popular also, as is bottled water, since the tap water may be a little salty. Coffee and tea are popular too, but perhaps due to the British heritage of the Bahamas, tea is often much better prepared than coffee.

INTERNET LINKS

https://www.nassauparadiseisland.com/authentic-bahamian-dishes
This travel site provides a quick overview of Bahamian cuisine with links and recipes.

https://www.thedailymeal.com/best-recipes/bahamian
This recipe site provides links to various Bahamian recipes on the internet.

PEAS 'N' RICE

This iconic Bahamian dish is sometimes made with the addition of chopped ham, coconut milk (in place of some of the liquid), and/or hot seasonings such as red pepper flakes. Many recipes call for a tablespoon of "browning," a Caribbean liquid seasoning that is something like Kitchen Bouquet or Worcestershire sauce, either of which can be substituted.

4 strips bacon, diced
1 medium onion, chopped
1 small green bell pepper, chopped
2 tablespoons tomato paste
Salt, pepper
Fresh thyme leaves stripped from
  3 or 4 sprigs
1 chopped fresh tomato
1 15-ounce (425.5 grams) can of
  pigeon peas, with liquid
1   ½ cups (285 g) uncooked
  long grain white rice
2 cups (475 milliliters) water

In a large saucepan or Dutch oven, fry bacon over medium heat until fat is rendered. Add onion and pepper and sauté until onion is translucent and bacon is cooked. Stir in tomato paste, pigeon peas and their liquid, chopped tomato, and fresh thyme.

Add rice, water, and salt and pepper to taste. Bring to a boil, cover, and lower heat. Simmer until liquid is absorbed and rice is cooked. Adjust seasonings to taste.

BIMINI COCONUT BREAD

Serve with guava jam for a real Bahamian treat.

2¼ teaspoons instant dry yeast
1 cup (240 mL) warm coconut milk
¼ cup (30 g) nonfat dry milk powder
⅓ cup (65 g) sugar
3 Tbsp honey
⅓ cup (80 mL) vegetable oil
1 tsp salt
3 eggs
3 Tbsp butter, softened
3—4 cups (360—440 g) all-purpose
  flour (plus extra, if needed)

In a large bowl, dissolve yeast in warm coconut milk. Add milk powder, sugar, honey, oil, salt, and eggs, and mix well.

Add butter and the flour, about ½ cup at a time, and mix until the dough pulls away from the sides of the mixing bowl and forms a ball.

On a lightly floured surface, knead dough until smooth and elastic, about 5 minutes.

Return the dough ball to bowl. Drizzle a bit of oil over the dough, coating the dough and sides of the bowl. Cover lightly with plastic wrap and let it rise in a warm place for about 2 hours or until about double in size.

Punch the dough down and form into 2 loaves. Place the loaves into 2 greased loaf pans. Cover with a kitchen towel and let rise for 1 hour.

Preheat the oven to 350°F (175°C). Bake the loaves for about 35 minutes or until golden brown.

Makes 2 loaves

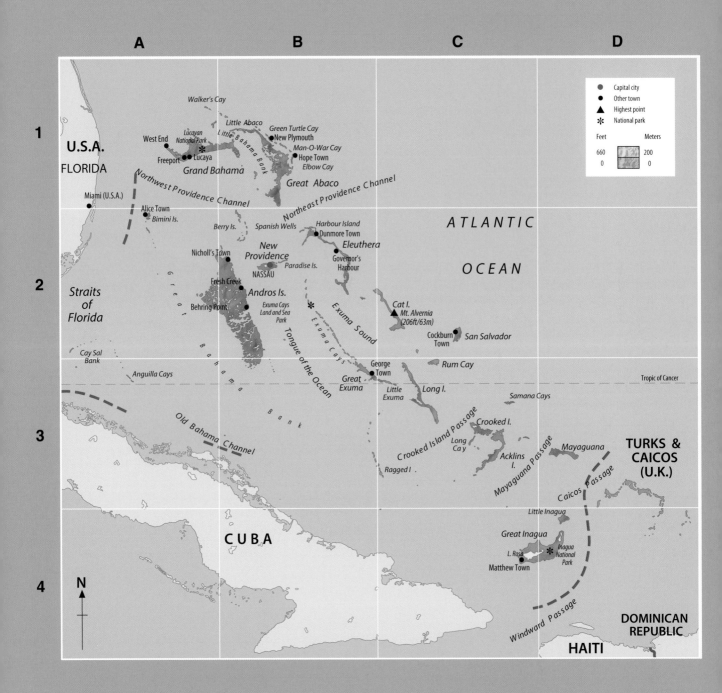

MAP OF BAHAMAS

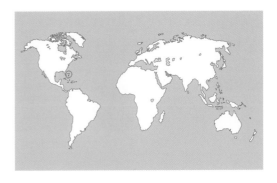

ECONOMIC BAHAMAS

Services

 Airport

 Port

 Tourism

Agriculture

 Citrus

 Poultry

 Vegetables

Natural Resources

 Aragonite

 Salt

 Timber

ABOUT THE ECONOMY

All figures are 2017 estimates unless otherwise stated.

GROSS DOMESTIC PRODUCT (GDP)
$11.64 billion (official exchange rate)

GDP PER CAPITA
$31,200

INFLATION RATE
1.4 percent

LABOR FORCE
196,900

UNEMPLOYMENT RATE
10 percent

POPULATION BELOW POVERTY LINE
14.8 percent

CURRENCY
$1 = 1 Bahamian $
The US dollar is maintained on par with the Bahamian dollar by the Central Bank of the Bahamas.

AGRICULTURE
Citrus, vegetables; poultry; seafood

NATURAL RESOURCES
Salt, aragonite, timber

MAIN INDUSTRIES
Tourism, banking, oil bunkering, maritime industries, transshipment and logistics, salt, aragonite, pharmaceuticals

MAIN EXPORTS
Rock lobster, aragonite, crude salt, polystyrene products

MAIN IMPORTS
Machinery and transportation equipment, chemicals, manufactured goods, mineral fuels, food, and live animals

MAIN TRADE PARTNER
United States

CULTURAL BAHAMAS

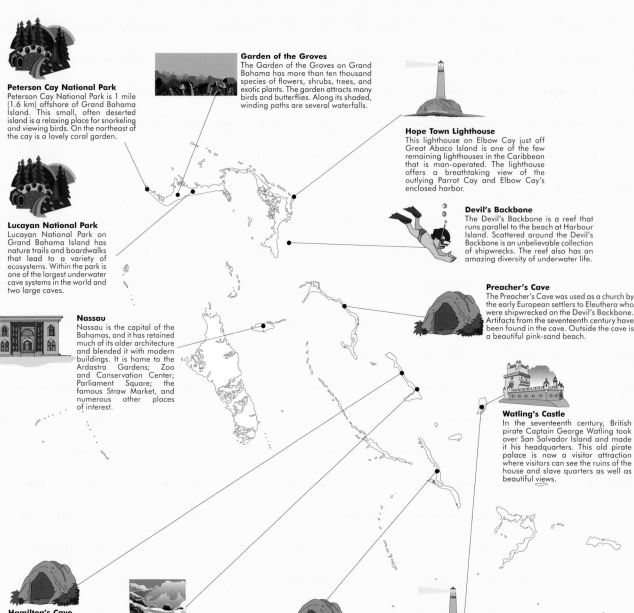

Peterson Cay National Park
Peterson Cay National Park is 1 mile (1.6 km) offshore of Grand Bahama Island. This small, often deserted island is a relaxing place for snorkeling and viewing birds. On the northeast of the cay is a lovely coral garden.

Lucayan National Park
Lucayan National Park on Grand Bahama Island has nature trails and boardwalks that lead to a variety of ecosystems. Within the park is one of the largest underwater cave systems in the world and two large caves.

Nassau
Nassau is the capital of the Bahamas, and it has retained much of its older architecture and blended it with modern buildings. It is home to the Ardastra Gardens; Zoo and Conservation Center; Parliament Square; the famous Straw Market, and numerous other places of interest.

Garden of the Groves
The Garden of the Groves on Grand Bahama has more than ten thousand species of flowers, shrubs, trees, and exotic plants. The garden attracts many birds and butterflies. Along its shaded, winding paths are several waterfalls.

Hope Town Lighthouse
This lighthouse on Elbow Cay just off Great Abaco Island is one of the few remaining lighthouses in the Caribbean that is man-operated. The lighthouse offers a breathtaking view of the outlying Parrot Cay and Elbow Cay's enclosed harbor.

Devil's Backbone
The Devil's Backbone is a reef that runs parallel to the beach at Harbour Island. Scattered around the Devil's Backbone is an unbelievable collection of shipwrecks. The reef also has an amazing diversity of underwater life.

Preacher's Cave
The Preacher's Cave was used as a church by the early European settlers to Eleuthera who were shipwrecked on the Devil's Backbone. Artifacts from the seventeenth century have been found in the cave. Outside the cave is a beautiful pink-sand beach.

Watling's Castle
In the seventeenth century, British pirate Captain George Watling took over San Salvador Island and made it his headquarters. This old pirate palace is now a visitor attraction where visitors can see the ruins of the house and slave quarters as well as beautiful views.

Hamilton's Cave
Hamilton's Cave on Long Island has artifacts and prehistoric cave drawings from the Lucayan tribe, the first known settlers in the Bahamas. Visitors can explore the ancient cave system, view historical cavern drawings, and see the remains and relics of the early history of the Bahamas.

Mount Alvernia
Mount Alvernia is the highest point in the Bahamas at 207 feet (63 m). At its peak stands the Hermitage, a medieval-style monastery built in 1939 by Father Jerome, a Roman Catholic priest who was also a skilled architect and sculptor.

Thunderball Grotto
Thunderball Grotto on Great Exuma Island was one of the sites used in the filming of two James Bond movies, *Thunderball* (1965) and *Never Say Never Again* (1983). Visitors at low tide can enjoy the abundant marine life.

Dixon Lighthouse
This lighthouse on San Salvador operates the old-fashioned way: it is fueled by kerosene that is pumped to the top to light the "mantle." Visitors can climb to the top of the 160-foot (49 m) structure, see the machinery, and get great views of the island.

ABOUT THE CULTURE

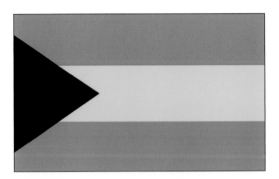

All figures are 2017 estimates unless otherwise stated.

OFFICIAL NAME
Commonwealth of the Bahamas

LAND AREA
5,382 square miles (13,939 sq km)

ESTIMATED TOTAL AREA
100,387 square miles (260,000 sq km)

CAPITAL
Nassau (on New Providence)

ISLANDS
700 inhabited islands and cays, approximately 2,000 uninhabited islets. Principal islands: New Providence, Grand Bahama; Family Islands: the Abacos (Great Abaco, Little Abaco), Acklins, Andros, Berry Island, the Biminis, Cat Island, Crooked Island, Eleuthera, the Exumas, Harbour Island, the Inaguas (Little Inagua, Great Inagua), Long Island, Mayaguana, Ragged Island, San Salvador, Spanish Wells, and Walker's Cay

HIGHEST POINT
Mount Alvernia (207 feet/63 m)

POPULATION
329,988

LIFE EXPECTANCY AT BIRTH
Total population: 72.6 years
Male: 70.2 years
Female: 75.1 years

BIRTHRATE
15.3 births/1,000 people

INFANT MORTALITY RATE
11.3 deaths/ 1,000 live births

ETHNIC GROUPS
Black 90.6 percent; white 4.7 percent; mixed race, black and white 2.1 percent; other 1.9 percent; unspecified 0.7 percent (2010 estimate)

RELIGION
Protestant 69.9 percent (includes Baptist 34.9 percent, Anglican 13.7 percent, Pentecostal 8.9 percent, Seventh Day Adventist 4.4 percent, Methodist 3.6 percent, Church of God 1.9 percent, Brethren 1.6 percent); Roman Catholic 12 percent; other Christian 13 percent (includes Jehovah's Witness 1.1 percent); other 0.6 percent; none 1.9 percent; unspecified 2.6 percent (2010 est.)

LANGUAGES
English (official), French Creole (among Haitian immigrants)

TIMELINE

IN BAHAMAS	IN THE WORLD
6000 BCE	
Evidence of the use of chili peppers in the Bahamas dates to this time.	**753 BCE** Rome is founded.
	1000 CE The Chinese perfect gunpowder and begin to use it in warfare.
1492 CE Christopher Columbus makes his first landing in the New World, in the Bahamas.	
1647 English and Bermudan religious refugees, the Eleutheran Adventurers, establish the first European settlement on the Bahamas.	
1666 Colonization of New Providence Island.	
1717 Bahamas becomes a British Crown colony.	
1783 Spain cedes the Bahamas to Britain in accordance with the Treaty of Paris after briefly occupying the islands the previous year.	**1776** US Declaration of Independence. **1789–1799** The French Revolution.
1834 Emancipation of slaves.	**1865** US Civil War begins.
	1939 World War II begins.
1940–1945 The Duke of Windsor—formerly King Edward VIII—serves as governor of the Bahamas.	
1955 Free-trade area is established in the town of Freeport, stimulating tourism and attracting offshore banking.	
1964 The Bahamas is granted internal autonomy.	
1967 Lynden Pindling becomes prime minister wins the islands' first legislative elections.	**1969** Neil Armstrong becomes the first human to walk on the moon.
1973 The Bahamas becomes independent.	

IN BAHAMAS	IN THE WORLD
1983 Government ministers face allegations of drug trafficking.	
1984 Pindling is endorsed as PLP leader after denying charges of corruption and ties to drug traffickers.	**1986** Nuclear power disaster at Chernobyl in Ukraine **1991** Breakup of the Soviet Union
1992 Hubert Ingraham becomes prime minister, ending twenty-five years of rule by Pindling.	
1996 Ingraham reinstates the death penalty.	**1997** Hong Kong is returned to China.
1998 Two convicted murderers are hanged despite international opposition over death penalty.	
2000 "Father of independence" Sir Lynden Pindling dies in August.	
2001 Dame Ivy Dumont in November becomes the Bahamas' first woman governor-general.	**2001** 9/11 terrorist attacks in the United States.
2002 Perry Christie becomes prime minister.	**2003** War in Iraq begins.
2006 UK-based court rules death sentence for murder breaches the Bahamian constitution.	
2007 Former prime minister Hubert Ingraham returns to office.	**2008** The first black president of the United States, Barack Obama, is elected. **2015–2016** ISIS launches terror attacks in Belgium and France.
2017 Swimming pigs of Pig Island found dead. Hubert Minis becomes prime minister.	**2017** Donald Trump becomes US president. Hurricanes devastate Houston, Caribbean islands, and Puerto Rico. **2018** Winter Olympics in South Korea

GLOSSARY

atoll
A ring-shape coral reef or a string of closely spaced small coral islands, enclosing or nearly enclosing a shallow lagoon.

Baja Mar
Spanish for "shallow sea," which refers to the sea surrounding the Bahamian islands.

chatting
Call-and-answer musical improvisation or ad-libbing in Bahamian musical folktales and spirituals. Also known as "rigging."

conch
Mollusk popular in the Bahamas as a snack (such as fritters), a main dish, and an ingredient in a salad.

Eleutheran Adventurers
English Puritans who in the seventeenth century traveled to Eleuthera to start a settlement where they could worship according to their own rules.

goombay
Music characterized by the rhythmic beat of goatskin drums along with other instruments including whistles, click sticks, cowbells, bongos, maracas, and conch-shell horns.

grits
Coarsely ground cornmeal.

Junkanoo
Festival between Christmas and New Year, featuring elaborate costumed parades and goombay bands and dancers.

Kalik
A Bahamian beer.

lukku-cairi
"Island people," Lucayans' name for themselves.

obeah
Bahamian tradition of spirit healing based on superstition and African religious beliefs.

rake 'n' scrape
Music made with instruments improvised from household implements and tools.

FOR FURTHER INFORMATION

BOOKS

Fodor's Travel. *Fodor's Bahamas*. Los Angeles: Internet Brands, 2018.

Lonely Planet. *The Bahamas*. New York: Lonely Planet, 2011.

ONLINE

Bahamas National Trust. https://bnt.bs.

Bahamas Online. www.thebahamas.com.

BBC News. Bahamas Country Profile. https://www.bbc.co.uk/news/world-latin-america-18722984.

BBC News. Timeline: Bahamas. http://news.bbc.co.uk/2/hi/americas/country_profiles/1166350.stm.

CIA World Factbook. The Bahamas. https://www.cia.gov/library/publications/resources/the-world-factbook/geos/bf.html

Encyclopaedia Britannica. The Bahamas. https://www.britannica.com/place/The-Bahamas.

Government of the Bahamas. http://www.bahamas.gov.bs.

Islands of the Bahamas. https://www.bahamas.com.

MUSIC

The Bahamas—Islands of Song. Smithsonian Folkways Recordings, 1997.

Cult Cargo: Grand Bahama Goombay. Numero, 2007.

Joseph Spence: The Complete Folkways Recordings, 1958. Smithsonian Folkways Recordings, 1992.

Kneeling Down Inside the Gate: The Great Rhyming Singers of the Bahamas. Rounder, 2009.

Religious Songs and Drums in the Bahamas. Smithsonian Folkways Recordings, 1953

BIBLIOGRAPHY

Bahamas.com. https://www.bahamas.com.

Blair, Jayson. "Lynden Pindling, 70, Who Led the Bahamas to Independence." *New York Times,* August 28, 2000. https://www.nytimes.com/2000/08/28/world/lynden-pindling-70-who-led-the-bahamas-to-independence.html.

Clemence, Sara. The $4 Billion Baha Mar Resort Is a Cacophony of Hospitality." *Bloomberg*, May 10, 2018. https://www.bloomberg.com/news/articles/2018-05-10/baha-mar-bahamas-resort-review.

Cooper, Abria. "Goombay Summer Festival 2018 begins July 5." *Freeport News*, July 3, 2018. http://thefreeportnews.com/news/goombay-summer-festival-2018-begins-july-5.

Eschner, Kay. "When Enslaved People Commandeered a Ship and Hightailed it to Freedom in the Bahamas." *Smithsonian Magazine*, November 7, 2017. https://www.smithsonianmag.com/smart-news/slave-revolt-ended-128-enslaved-people-free-bahamas.

Johnson, Scott. "Post-Irma, Parrots in the Abaco Pinelands Are Holding Their Own." Birdscaribbean.org, May 29, 2018. https://www.birdscaribbean.org/2018/05/post-irma-parrots-in-the-abaco-pinelands-are-holding-their-own.

Keith, Donald. "Nothing Short of Miraculous." *Times of the Islands*, Fall 2012. http://www.timespub.tc/2012/10/nothing-short-of-miraculous.

Robles, Frances. "Immigration Rules in Bahamas Sweep Up Haitians." *New York Times*, January 30, 2015. https://www.nytimes.com/2015/01/31/world/haitians-are-swept-up-as-bahamas-tightens-immigration-rules.html

Ruggerio, Nina. "Everything to Know About Swimming with Pigs in the Bahamas." *Travel & Leisure*, May 19, 2017. https://www.travelandleisure.com/trip-ideas/bahamas-swimming-pigs-big-major-cay

Smith, Larry. "The Very Strange World of Gambling in the Bahamas." *Bahama Pundit*, August 8, 2012. http://www.bahamapundit.com/2012/08/the-very-strange-world-of-gambling-in-the-bahamas.html

Soodalter, Ron. "Murder In Paradise: Sir Harry Oakes, the Bahamian Yankee." *Portland Monthly*, Summerguide 2017. https://www.portlandmonthly.com/portmag/2017/06/murder-in-paradise-sir-harry-oakes-the-bahamian-yankee.

Tan, Jim. "Queen Conch Dying Out in the Bahamas Despite Marine Parks." *Mongabay*, February 2018. https://news.mongabay.com/2018/02/queen-conch-dying-out-in-the-bahamas-despite-marine-parks

Tribune 242. "Bahama Parrot Population Back on the Rise in Inagua," September 18, 2013. http://www.tribune242.com/news/2013/sep/18/bahama-parrot-population-back-on-the-rise-in.

Woodward, Colin. "The Last Days of Blackbeard." *Smithsonian*, February 2014. https://www.smithsonianmag.com/history/last-days-blackbeard-180949440.

INDEX

INDEX